THE
DAD
DIALOGUES

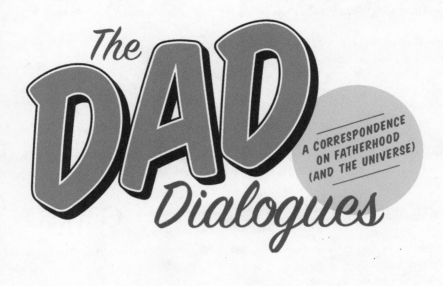

The **DAD** *Dialogues*

A CORRESPONDENCE ON FATHERHOOD (AND THE UNIVERSE)

GEORGE BOWERING

&

CHARLES DEMERS

ARSENAL PULP PRESS
VANCOUVER

ARSENAL PULP PRESS
Suite 202 – 211 East Georgia St.
Vancouver, BC V6A 1Z6
Canada
arsenalpulp.com

The publisher gratefully acknowledges the support of the Canada Council for the Arts and the British Columbia Arts Council for its publishing program, and the Government of Canada (through the Canada Book Fund) and the Government of British Columbia (through the Book Publishing Tax Credit Program) for its publishing activities.

   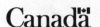

Photographs throughout courtesy of Jean Baird, Thea Bowering, George Bowering, Cara Ng-Demers, and Charles Demers
Photos on pages 147 and 221 taken by Lynn Spink

Cover Illustration by Bob McPartlin
Cover and text design by Oliver McPartlin
Edited by Susan Safyan

Printed and bound in Canada

Library and Archives Canada Cataloguing in Publication:
 Bowering, George, 1935-
[Correspondence. Selections]
      The dad dialogues : a correspondence on fatherhood (and the universe)
/ George Bowering, Charles Demers.

Issued in print and electronic formats.
ISBN 978-1-55152-662-1 (paperback).—ISBN 978-1-55152-663-8 (html)

      1. Bowering, George, 1935- —Correspondence. 2. Demers, Charles,
1980- —Correspondence. 3. Authors, Canadian (English)—Correspondence.
4. Fatherhood. I. Demers, Charles, 1980- . Correspondence. Selections.
II. Title. III. Title: Correspondence. Selections.

PS8503.O875Z48 2016   C816'.54   C2016-904379-7
                                                C2016-904380-0

We would like to acknowledge the priceless contribution of the moms.

The Baby Daughter Book:
George's Version

One of the most enjoyable things about the 2013 baseball season was watching the great stand-up guy Charlie Demers sit down at Nat Bailey Stadium to watch our beloved Single-A short season Vancouver Canadians and start learning the wonderful and secret things that make baseball such a marvelous thing to pay attention to.

A neat thing about baseball is the pace. Instead of standing up and spilling beer on the people in front of you and screaming obscenities at players and officials, you have time to carry on discussions with each other, all the while letting one eye rove around the stands to check on cute children and adults.

Among the conversations that naturally arose from time to time was the artistic and progressive pregnancy of Cara Ng, the fabled wife of Mr Demers. During the season, Cara was not all that noticeably pregnant, partly because she is a petite person and partly because she is sort of inscrutable. (That's a jest, folks.) Of course, one of the things you often think about while sitting at the Nat is: I wonder what I should write a book about? Jean Baird, the effulgent second wife of George Bowering, said, "Why don't you two writer/comedians compose a book about becoming and learning to be fathers of daughters? You can build it out of letters between you, the old fart who became a father in 1971, and the tyro who is expecting to do so just before Christmas of 2013."

"What?" I said. "Have I not already collaborated with other writers, some of them way younger than I? Am I not already working on a number of books, contrary to the advice of Jack Spicer, the great San Francisco poet, who urged that you pay full attention to one project at a time? Don't I have so much to do that at mid-afternoon every day I am still sitting at a keyboard though dressed in jammies and housecoat?"

"Sure, okay," said Charlie. "Let's do it."

The Baby Daughter Book: Charlie's Version

Here's how I remember it:

A first pregnancy is a span of time that the expectant parents spend in equal parts soliciting and dodging advice from everyone they meet. I can't speak for the words of wisdom imparted by women to my wife, Cara, but I can say that in general, the insights offered by men to nearly-fathers tend on the whole to be fairly poor. For the most part, they're animated by a rank-pulling sadism or empathetic masochism, and offers of, "Well, you'd better sleep now while you can!" predominate the counselling like cheap peanuts in a can of mixed nuts.

Thankfully, this was not the kind of advice that I got from George Bowering on the specific subject of being a father to a daughter while in the stands at Nat Bailey Stadium as we watched the Vancouver Canadians play baseball. His guidance had been solicited, both because I very much love and respect George, and also because the longer you can keep him talking at a baseball game, the fewer things he can yell at people, including children, who demonstrate (usually by means of enthusiastic exuberance) an ignorance about the sport (woe betide the section that cheers when the home team catches a sacrifice fly).

The game took place at a point in Cara's pregnancy when the stack of books about parenting was growing at our house, and as George wrapped up a helpful anecdote about raising his daughter Thea—throwing a bit of light onto what would be my duties in relation to my then-unnamed and unborn little girl—it occurred to me that of the more than 100 books he had written, the only genre he hadn't yet published in was "how-to parenting guide."

"You should write a book about parenting," I said, just as the in-

stinct for self-preservation kicked in, and I realized that for no reason whatsoever, I was writing myself out of the idea. "I mean, *we*
should write a book about parenting."

There in the stands, likely before the inning was even finished,
George, Jean, and I hashed out the rough, epistolary scheme for the
book you are reading. I watched the rest of the game with a deep
and abiding satisfaction, realizing the magnitude of the gift I'd just
arranged for my baby daughter: a record of the first parts of her life,
a book co-written in her honour by one of Canada's most celebrated,
beloved, and talented men of letters. *And* George Bowering!

Dear George,

I'm writing you this first letter from Halifax, which is a swell town that has very nice people in it, is very easy to walk around, and where I happen to be a full four hours closer to becoming a father than I would be at home, on Pacific Standard Time. We're one month, one week away from the due date (minus four hours, depending on where one happens to be).

The last time I flew into Halifax was this past April, the day after we found out that Cara was pregnant. We had been trying to conceive for four or five months by that point, and in that ridiculously short window we'd run the full gamut from fertile overconfidence to despondent conviction of our sterility. The first month, we ran out to buy pregnancy tests almost a week before Cara's period was due; by springtime, Cara was back to sipping wine and I, idiotically, was asking the doctor if I could go get my sperm count checked. (In fairness, I've been studying for that test very rigorously for a long time.) Eventually, we settled into the long odds against pregnancy. Dr Wong, our GP, told us to have sex every other day, since the chances of conception were best on the day of ovulation and the forty-eight hours on either side. The odds on those best-chance days? One in five.

By April 17, it was still a bit premature to bring out any test-strips to desecrate, but since I was leaving the next day for the Halifax Comedy Festival—which I'd been hoping for years to get into, since it would let my own father show me off in his adoptive city—I begged Cara to give it a go. On the off chance that we were pregnant, I didn't want to find out alone, on the other side of the country, with no one with whom I could share the still-delicate news.

She went upstairs, and I could hear the answer in the awkward

"Um ..." she let go as she came back down carrying a results-bar struck through not the once we'd grown accustomed to, but twice, indicating that we needed to start saving for somebody else's tuition. I ripped the business end off the pregnancy test and kept the results with me in my carry-on, taking the test out every now and again to marvel at it on the plane. I had promised Cara that I wouldn't tell anybody anything. The pregnancy test would be my strength, the talisman that would give me the power I needed to hold in the news.

I lasted until the 20th or the 21st, which is pretty impressive in retrospect. It was a Saturday or a Sunday, but let's call it a Sunday, since I'd like to believe that I was at least able to hold it in long enough that I didn't make the announcement on Hitler's birthday.

My dad, his husband (you knew about that, right?), and I had driven up to Peggy's Cove for the afternoon, and with our Atlantic-misted faces squinting into the beautiful view, I couldn't resist the moment. Cara wasn't too mad.

The current visit to Halifax isn't shaping up to be quite as much fun; this time, I'm here because of chemotherapy, not comedy. Dad's formerly low-grade lymphoma made a bit of a jump in aggressivity over the summer, and I've arrived just after the sixth of six installments of treatment. His hair has already started to grow back, but it's soft. Almost twenty-five years ago, chemo took away my mother's beautiful, wavy red hair and replanted it with kinky, brown-grey curls that were hers for the remaining five years of her life.

My dad seems to be doing well (though he looks more like my grandmother than I've ever noticed before, and where he used to be about only an inch shorter than me, he's now two, though I don't think that can be chalked up to the chemo). We'll have an idea of where things will go from here by the end of December, when he's just started into his career as a grandfather. He's optimistic, but he always is, and if I'm pessimistic, it's only because I always am. He's been responding very well to his treatment so far. All I can tell you is that I hope dearly and more than a little desperately that my tenures as a son and as a dad have a very long and significant overlap.

People keep asking if I'm nervous about the baby, and I always feel like I'm disappointing them when I say no. I feel like it's what they hope for and expect. People want to see a big fat pregnant lady and a terrified father-to-be; it's part of the romantic spectacle of anticipating the baby. But as a couple, we've let them down on both scores. At eight-and-a-half months, Cara's gained twelve pounds, which is about the difference I manage before and after Thanksgiving dinner. And as for me—a man who, since childhood, has located sources of worry both legitimate and illegitimate in order to create a never-ending and ever-escalating lifelong crescendo of anxiety about every single thing in the universe—I am inexplicably cool as a cucumber with regards to baby. There's nothing but thrilled, happy, slightly impatient waiting. The best we can offer the world is a big fat man who, while not strictly pregnant, is expecting, and is nervous about everything else.

Incidentally: though Georgine was never on the table as a name, I can promise you that Georgette was considered very seriously and sincerely before falling out of contention.

Love,
Charlie

Dear Charlie,

I imagine that when you read this you are going to be in the Halifax airport on your way home. The last time I was there, there was a Hello Kitty kiosk in the middle of the concourse. I don't know whether you know that I sort of collect Hello Kitty stuff, and I don't know whether you are going to let little Georgette have Hello Kitty stuff, but I thought that I would just tip you off, in case. I know how easy it is to pass by a display of Hello Kitty stuff without noticing.

I don't know about due dates. Thea was a little late, according to hers. But I can tell you where I was one month and one week before her birth. August 31, 1971 was Traditional Pub Night, which was celebrated every Tuesday at the Cecil Hotel in Vancouver. Writers all across the country knew that Tuesday nights were their opportunity to meet and buy beer for their Vancouver counterparts. In familiar parlance it was called "Lodge Night." The commissioner of TPN, poet George Stanley, also dubbed Wednesdays "No Shoulds Day." This particular TPN was the last night of twenty-cent beer. On the morrow, a glass would cost a quarter of a dollar.

Your GP is Dr Wong? My heart specialist is Dr Wong. My GP is Dr Chong. My eye guy is Dr Stong. When I broke my hip, my orthopedic surgeon was Dr Song. I hope you will not mind if I try to delay needing an oncologist. Sorry.

We never had any trouble with conception. Actually, Angela and I were childless for the first nine years of our marriage. When we got married, we agreed not to have any kids for five years. At the end of five years, I wasn't ready to be a father. Then when I considered it, Angela wasn't ready to be a mom because she wanted to be a student. But on the last night of 1970, in Montreal, we never got around to going to the party across the street from our apartment because we were lying on the living room floor and listening to music. Angela was between flights to the west coast, where her father was very ill. So you see, we too were thinking of the cycle of life, even though we did not know that a new one was starting.

Sure, I knew about your dad, knew that he was in a new marriage, and I had gathered some sense of his medical history. Of course you want to be a son and a dad concurrently for a long time. One of my favourite family snapshots is one of my dad holding one-week-old Thea on his lap. This picture was taken in our rented house on York Street, the one that had been a commune until recently. My dad was sixty-four years old, newly retired from his science teaching job in the Okanagan. He and Thea saw each other a few times before my dad passed away a little more than two years later.

Speaking of pictures: if this is going to be a dads' baby book, there will naturally be a lot of pictures, eh? Now, this isn't really fair, because when Thea was a baby you had to buy film and get the film developed and all that stuff you would probably be mystified by in your take-a-hundred-digital-pictures-and-save-the-best-ones era.

As I said, we never worried about conception, so I know nothing about testing for pregnancy—but doesn't a bunny have to die? I don't remember anything about ultrasounds (I know, the first snapshots in your album) and all that stuff. But I do remember "birth class." One evening every week (not Tuesday, of course), we would jump into my poor old Chevrolet and drive across the Lions Gate Bridge and up Taylor Way to St. David's United Church for our birth class.

You have to remember that 1971 occurred in the late sixties, when you were supposed to be hip about everything. The commune that Thea spent her prenatal months in had a lot of rules and enthusiasms, having to do with where we shopped, how many languages we had Mao's *Little*

Red Book in, and what psychedelic plants grew in the back yard. It was a time of cults and alliances that sprang from the various liberations that made us so hopeful about the future of, say, kids born in 1971.

Our birth classes were organized around the Lamaze technique, a method that originated in France, where Dr Fernand Lamaze had the idea of empowering pregnant women to take charge of their own pregnancies. Medical intervention would be replaced by exercises in breathing and massage and movements that would train a woman to handle pain and anxiety. Some more radical groups would add underwater birth to the process.

So women and their partners learned to breathe together, the little panting breaths that helped the mother-to-be become an artist rather than a patient. The fathers in that room had facial hair—it was 1971—and the mothers wore loose-fitting clothes in earth colours. I was a sophisticated and ironic poet and scholar who knelt on the church basement floor, surrounded by unembarrassed women's reproductive bodies. We panted. We partners massaged the smalls of our large women's backs.

On the drive back to Kitsilano, Angela and I and the encased baby listened to CBC radio because it still played adult music and discussion back then.

I had been talked into the Lamaze system as I was talked into so many things back then. But I think that the group feeling of those nights in West Vancouver helped me with my nervousness. Like you, I am a nervous Nellie. I don't think I was as calm as you are in the last month or two of pregnancy, but the fact that I was kind of taking part in one helped a lot.

Over and out,
GB

Dear George,

I don't think that I would be living up to my responsibilities as the white father of a half-Chinese-Canadian girl if I didn't allow her to have Hello Kitty. She will get Hello Kitty, *tarte au sucre*, and, say, Scotch whiskey. Those are her multifarious birthrights.

Hello Kitty did bite me in the ass when I tried to be a big shot a year or so back with my nephew, Griffin—future cousin to my baby girl. Griffin was and is a very shy boy, very slow to warm up to anybody, and one always starts again from zero at every new visit. We had gone out for dim sum at a Hong Kong-style mall in Richmond and, very patiently, over the course of the meal, I had coaxed him out of his shell (babies love dim sum, incidentally). Afterward, I was carrying him through the mall and took him into the Hello Kitty shop to show him around. With his tiny hand, he reached out and grabbed a small, pink doll from the shelf, and I decided to seize the moment to show that Uncle Charlie was the kind of uncle who makes things happen—what my nephew wants, he gets! Anyway, the goddamn thing was like fifty bucks. If he's ever played with it, I've never been a witness.

The thought of childbirth and a prenatal culture steeped in communal, utopian optimism, as you've described, is incredibly exotic to me. I know that's hard to believe, coming from a lifelong Lotuslander, but keep in mind that I was born the same year as the Reagan presidency, 1980—basically the year the door closed on the idea of making the world better for anything but markets, when any emancipation that went beyond the individual body or bank account became suspect. It seems to me that, however sweet it is, childbirth has become the ultimate, accessorizable performance by the neoliberal body. So many of the parents I know are in a crazy status-race to have the most idiosyncratic possible birth (you haven't really had a baby till you've delivered into a hand-crafted, artisanal kiddie-pool in a purpose-built cottage in the forest with a roof thatched by a team of Cuban doulas) that sometimes I feel like a hillbilly when I tell folks we're having the baby delivered by our doctor, in a hospital. As my friend Erica says, "You just *have* to have a free-range baby."

I'm so used to babymaking as a yuppie performance, in fact, that I was totally knocked on my heels to see the roughneck dads at the Babies Я Us in Halifax when I went shopping with my dad last week. But not as shocked as I was by the baby lingerie that was on sale at Sears right across from the strollers—wildly disturbing, leopard-print spandex panties for very small people, whose tag declaimed that they were a "Girl Thing." It looked like something out of the Jimmy Savile Collection. I may be relatively calm about becoming a dad, but this stuff? This stuff terrifies me. First person to give us animal-print panties for the baby is getting a punch in the nose.

Not that my generation has gotten the short end of the stick on all of it: I don't mind telling you, you missed out on ultrasounds. We got the first one at around nine weeks, I think, and I just flipped for it—this little grey jumping bean she was, and I started to cry with joy. We got another one at nineteen weeks, where we got to see baby's beautiful profile (which nevertheless only fuelled more and fiercer debate about whose nose she was going to have), but I've attached for you my favourite of the ultrasounds, a picture of the bottom of her feet. My kid's feet. Soon to be shod in little Hello Kitty sneakers.

Love,
C.

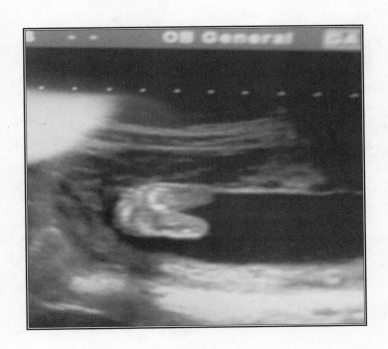

Dear Charlie,

I was moved, as they say, by your remarks on 1980, by the difference between our world in which we thought that at last we were headed for a democratic future, maybe that the Vietnam war and the US assassinations were the last horrible thickets to break through, and your world (where I am forced to live now, with regret) in which strangers Taser each other at Black Friday shopathons. In 1971, we thought that we were bringing a child into a world that would be freer than ours, where people would give things to one another instead of setting up no-fly zones.

Exactly two months before our daughter was born there was an event called the Gastown Riot. Mounted Vancouver police rode through a crowd, swinging their long American clubs and smashing heads. The mayor, frothing and wild-eyed as he often was, appeared on television approving his employees' actions. What seemed significant to us young idealists was that the bourgeois media called it a "police riot." They were led by the CTV coverage, in which the constabulary were called "thugs."

My daughter is a little older than you, but she has had to grow up in your world too. The number-one hit song of 1971, the year she was born, was "Joy to the World" by Three Dog Night. Sure, Jeremiah was a bullfrog, not a gangsta.

So I roll my eyes and snap my fingers and take it to heart when you mention Frederick's of Holy Shit underwear for little girl tots. Just the other day I crumpled up the newspaper and tried to remember my breathing exercises when I saw an ad for little children's clothing headed by the line: "Dress them for success." Oh, and while you're at it, put a nice woolen coat on your fuzzy little dog.

Please! Decking baby Madison or Mackenzie out in slut garb? Then taking a thousand pictures on your cellphone to put among the meals and kittens on Facebook? I do remember once buying Wonder Woman underwear for my kid, but she was ten or so and reading books. For one thing, the kid understood camp and irony. For another thing, Wonder Woman is no slut. Merciful Minerva! I wonder whether Madison's mother knows who Minerva is?

But I know that baby Georgina is going to have smart, responsible, democratic, hip, educated parents. She is going to grin ironically whenever she gets a new Hello Kitty item, and she is going to figure it out about pink.

Well, my birthday happened two days ago, and there was no natal news from your house, so I am assuming that your daughter will not share my date of birth. But we do know that she is pretty well a shoe-in to share my month. Until then we will just have to be satisfied with that picture of pretty little bare Ng feet.

Love,
GB
P.S.: I know it is "shoo." I just wanted to introduce you to the world of puns.

Dear George,

I happened to read your most recent letter after spending an hour or two with the news of Nelson Mandela's death, which had the effect of drawing out the world-historical themes you touched upon even more starkly. President Obama went on TV to say that Mandela had "bent the arc of the moral universe toward justice," which seemed like an oddly muscular extrapolation from MLK's phrase. Then again, who knows—maybe Obama's right, and the arc doesn't bend toward justice but rather needs to be bent. Your letter certainly doesn't lend itself to the idea that things have a natural way of getting better.

The optimism you describe yourself as having had before Thea's birth reminds me of the optimism my parents had before mine (or so I've been told—I had to take their word for it). Coming at the end of a very hot decade in the relationship between Canada and Quebec (but not the good kind of hot), my birth to one Francophone and one Anglophone parent just a little over a month after the first referendum—on Canada Day, no less—was cause for retrospectively quaint optimism, particularly on the part of my Anglophone mother.

Here's an idea that I comfort myself with, and I'm fairly convinced that it's not 100-percent delusional: In the same way that you and my parents seemed to have every reason to be hopeful for the world your children would be brought up in, only to be let down, maybe my despairing expectations for the times my daughter's going to live in will also be upended. I'm comforted by the people who've started bucking against the consensus—Idle No More, the Québec student strikers, the Occupy Movement—and who knows? Maybe they'll help save us. Either that or the Pacific Ocean will turn to acid, flood the streets, and melt the Hello Kitty shoes right off my girl's cute little feet. You know, either-or.

From the world-historical to the infinitesimally personal: this past week, I've had to confront the fact that maybe I'm feeling more sub-terranean anxiety about becoming a dad than I'd realized. I snapped at Cara a few times—not something to be proud of at any time, re-ally, but especially shameful when one's partner is swollen up with a soon-to-be person—setting off dumb yelling matches about carpet cleaning and travel mugs (so at least I've got my priorities straight). Luckily, I was able to apologize and reel it in when I figured out what was happening, not to mention taking a bit of pharmaceutical help for my panic. Cara was forgiving, without totally letting me off the hook. Ever since she learned about oxytocin, the "love hormone" that will occasionally flood her with warm feelings for baby and father before, during, and after labour, she lets me know when I'm on thin ice by saying, "My oxytocin levels are getting low ..."

We've done a lot of very parent-ish stuff since my last letter. Along with maybe ten other expectant couples, we did a tour of the maternity ward at the hospital where we're having the baby. It was a mixed experience, from a comedian's perspective. At one point, Cara was holding up the elevator while she went to get a bottle of water; apologetically, I turned to the rest of the tour and said, "Sorry, my wife is pregnant." Nothing. But I won the crowd back over in the de-livery room, when the nurse showed us the laughing gas and I asked if we could try it. What can I say? Some audiences have no time for subtlety, they just want drug material.

Over the weekend and on Monday, we did a prenatal crash course. It was seven or eight couples on the ground floor of a Vancouver Spe-cial quite close to our place, plus the instructor, who works as a dou-la. On the whole, the classes were pretty helpful, and the people were really great. I guess the kinds of men who are willing to do a three-day prenatal course tend to be pretty okay guys on the whole, and the mothers were very pleasant, and of course, being deeply pregnant, all looked very beautiful, with thick shiny hair and glowing faces.

There was a lot of emphasis on "instinct," which seemed like an odd theme to hit so hard upon in a class that took three days and wasn't, you know, free. We heard many times that "your body knew how to grow this baby, and it knows how to deliver it," which ought to come as news to the bajillion women who've died in childbirth over the past gazillion years. My psychologist tells me that she deals with many new mothers whose anxieties are cranked sky-high by the way they're pressured to be perfect parents, and looking around our class, I could see it happening. That part was awful; mouths downturned in guilty foreboding at any talk of C-sections or epidurals—God forgive any of these moms who have to be cut open or can't breastfeed, because from the looks on their faces, they won't be able to forgive themselves.

The class was officially non-judgmental, but with an easily detected undercurrent of suspicion toward the medical establishment. I find a lot of this tiresome, but we've got a great doctor. I did get angry, however, when the instructor said, "At two or three months, some of you will choose to have your babies immunized ..." I didn't get the feeling that she was setting up the end of the sentence, which should have been "while others will be grossly irresponsible from both a private and public health perspective." On Monday night, we learned about the seemingly endless benefits of breastfeeding and saw a pretty outrageously adorable video of little babies rooting for and latching onto their mothers' nipples. Our instructor said that if we wanted to see more videos like it, we should Google "breast crawl" to find footage of newborns making their ways from mommies' tummies to their chests. I ventured that those search terms would probably also yield some less wholesome offerings from the Internet.

Over the past week, I've found myself overwhelmingly bored with baby talk, which seems to ping between two poles: consumer baby-product choices, and surreptitiously judgmental birthing and child-rearing stories. It's one of those things where it's no one person, but the sheer weight of all of them together—the 9,000th person to jocularly say, "Better stock up on sleep now, buddy, hyuk, hyuk!"—that grinds one under the monotony.

On Sunday night, I decided to escape the whole discourse and went to see my friends in a play. I happened to be seated next to my neighbour, Andrew, of whom I am incredibly fond, but who almost immediately began telling me about how great he and his wife's doula was—a doula who turned out, by coincidence, to be the instructor from our prenatal class. The entire thing reached new levels of ubiquity when Andrew started into an analogy for what a doula does (it involved lifeguards and swimming instructors), when the non-black woman with dreadlocks who was sitting in front of us turned around enthusiastically and gushed, "*I'm* a doula!"

For the time being, it seems, there is no getting away from it.

Love,
C.

Dear Charlie,

Don't work on more than one thing at a time. I have long adopted that advice as a rule, though I might once in a while make a note about an idea that could turn into a book or something. However, I seem now, in my decrepitude, to have slipped into the habit of working on five or six books at a time. On top of that, I seem to have a date just about every day to see one of my many doctors or old friends. For example, I have just come from lunch with my old friends and publishers Karl and Christy Siegler, who have sold their Vancouver condo and are headed back up the coast. All this by way of explaining why it is that nearly a week might go by between your letter and my reply. Well, all right. That was pretty normal before the advent of e-"mail." Oh, and if this were another kind of project, I might have told you what all those books are that I am writing.

I might also clean up my prose sentences.

I will ignore the fact that you continue to refer to the creature inside Cara as "my daughter" rather than "Georgette," and proceed to address my attention to your reverse-psychology of future history, wherein you propose that your pessimism will be unrealized because some young-ish humans have decided to be idle no more and to occupy the spaces that we were afraid were being abandoned by pale striplings staring at games on their iPhones. (How's that for a sentence?) Jean said to me one day last year that she agrees with whoever said that we will have to be saved by the Aboriginal peoples around the world. Could be. They certainly seem a better bet than the political hypocrites who sat in the dry parts of the big stadium at Madiba's celebration of life in South Africa this week.

I myself am generally sad about the way that most people are now more concerned with their utility bills than they are with protecting the planet and its inhabitants, but I am somewhat encouraged that the parents of the newly born are going to be people such as Cara and you. I'd be happy to put little G. in your hands. I hope that the maniacs in the US Congress cannot prevail if you angels keep your ears and eyes open.

On the personal front, your most important sentence was "Cara was forgiving, without totally letting me off the hook." Very good news—if she had been unforgiving, or totally forgiving, your relationship might have had a dent in it. In either case, you could have just gone ahead and been an arsehole. But with her very wise, maybe instinctually wise (if that is possible) response, she has let you know that the Charles Demers she likes is welcome and needed in the family. How did you get so lucky? Aw, you have probably asked yourself that from time to time. But further on that: Cara is showing you how to be a dad, which is good to know around this time.

Now, I didn't know about that oxytocin business, and I am always a tad suspicious of new words that sound a little wellness-oriented. But I have felt the male version of that inside glow or flood you refer to as the "love hormone." In a few months, when the baby cries or otherwise cuts right through the time that would have been perfect, small as it is, to write a paragraph or two for your real life, and you are already late in preparing a class, and you don't have clean socks or gonch because the machines are full of baby items, and you are on the second day of the rice leftovers that you chew while trying to keep awake at the desk—that love flood is going to steam up your famous eyeglasses, Chas.

I have to say that I don't really get your comedic tour of the hospital. I thought that your remark at the elevator was funny, and would have chuckled, but the laughing gas business didn't get a laugh out of me. Maybe I am just more sophisticated than your usual birth-class crowd. Come to think of it, I do not recall a lot of humorous badinage in our Lamaze classes. Of course we believed that we were still young progressive people; maybe the other people in the class did not agree with me that young progressive people have superior humour. Maybe most people who are approaching the births of their first babies just don't find the world funny. Maybe that is why I didn't laugh out loud when I first saw my daughter's feet. I did remark on their size and colour, though.

I had to look up "doula." I guess that what was happening when we were getting ready for the blessed or scary event was that we husbands or partners were being trained to be something like doulas. We would be there doing breathing with our wives, giving our wives back massages, murmuring or shouting reminders of the routine of assisted natural childbirth, and so on. I was reminded of my friend Sergio Mondragón, who was the husband of my friend Margaret Randall, the poet. This was in Mexico City in 1964. Sergio was a yoga instructor as well as a poetry publisher, and while Margaret was pregnant with Ximena Mondragón y Randall, they did breathing and exercises and imaging together. When Meg's ten-month gestation was over, a bunch of us poets, English-speaking and Spanish-speaking, went to the hospital run by women refugees from Franco's Spain, and had a birth party. There must have been a dozen of us around Meg's bed, and when Meg and Sergio went into the delivery room, we partied on until we heard a little wail, whereupon we went to the viewing space and greeted the new Mexican citizen.

I share your feeling about the competition to be perfect mothers (and fathers) with perfect children delivered perfectly. Our classes were aimed at natural childbirth, and there was a kind of smugness going around. It was something like the vibrations coming off earth people who found a way to let you know that they didn't wear leather belts. It was better than the sight of a girl in a private school uniform stepping out of a BMW SUV, but we could have done five-percent better without it. And I am glad that Angela received a little needle after many hours on the delivery level of the hospital's Willow Pavilion.

Here's a little non-historical note. On July 6, 1971, one month short of his seventieth birthday and three months before Thea's birth, Louis Armstrong died. He was one of my heroes when I was a small-town boy. Three months to the day before I was born, Seiji Ozawa was born. What famous musical person was born exactly three months before you were? Or your kid, G?

Love,
GB

December 20, 2013

Dear George,

Let's not be too hard on my laughing gas joke; you have to allow for timing and delivery—two concepts with which I happen to be obsessed right now, two days out from our due date.

(Parenthetically [literally]: Now it's my turn to offer an explanation for the lag time between letters, except that I don't have one besides things just generally being crazy—a legitimate excuse I have gotten used to lately, but seeing as things probably won't be letting up much over the next ten to eighteen years or so, I'd better figure out a way to deal with craziness. How does one do it? How did you write and teach and grow a moustache and stuff, all while being a dad?)

I just came in from outside, which is covered in a thick, rare Vancouver snow. In a pretty fatherly move, if I may say so, I took some time to brush the snow off the car, as well as to shovel and salt a pathway out into the street in case we find ourselves having to leave for the hospital tonight. In equally fatherly fashion, my lower back started wonking out just a bit, so I came back inside and lay down flat on the floor with an ice-pack. I shovelled more than I strictly had to, but it felt good to set myself some sort of physical task to prepare for labour, rather than just sitting inside with the anxious anticipation going off inside me like Drāno. It's such a strange position to be in, to know that this monumentally life-changing physical process, which will more than likely wreak havoc on one's beloved, is imminent (and that "imminent" means sometime between ten seconds and a week and a half from now). This is tough. I can't remember who said this, me or my psychologist, but adrenaline doesn't work well on a simmer.

That's one hell of a beautiful story about baby Ximena. It's an unreal feeling to know that some time, any minute now, Cara and I will be in the middle of living a story we'll be telling, like that one, decades hence. You know when you sometimes have the sharp sensation that—*contra* Francis Fukuyama—you're experiencing an historical moment? These past few days, I have this very self-conscious awareness of living in personal history. We had a snowy walk around Trout Lake today, right by our place, and I took some photos and video of the two of us with my phone, for posterity's sake. And whenever something like that happens, I find myself imagining that maybe this is the way the story of the night she was born will start. It's a strange sense of being both inside a moment and observing oneself in it at the same time.

Like this: with any luck, this'll be the last letter I send to you before I become a dad. Or maybe it won't be. So how do I carry myself?

Oh, in answer to your question: according to the Wikipedia page *http://en.wikipedia.org/wiki/List_of_deaths_in_rock_and_roll*, nobody died three months before I came into the world. But Bon Scott, AC/DC's original lead singer, died of alcohol poisoning about five months before I came along, and the month and a half before I was born, Joy Division's Ian Curtis hanged himself, and Carl Radle of Derek and the Dominos died of a kidney infection. And, of course, less than half a year after I was born, Mark Chapman gunned down John Lennon. This is awful. How did we get to talking about this? Oh, wait—you didn't ask about deaths. You asked about births. The singer Jessica Simpson was born nine days after I was, on July 10, 1980, and Christina Aguilera was born that December. A more cynical, less sensitive, generally more horrible person than me might point out that 1980's births and deaths had about the same net effect on the world of music.

I also loved Louis Armstrong when I was a kid. I was a trumpet player too, but never practised and, generally, stank. The great Lou Reed, who passed on in October, will certainly be remembered as the biggest loss from the musical world this year. And as for "what famous musical person was born exactly three months" before my kid—well, I guess we'll have to wait and see, right?

Love,
C.

December 25, 2013

Dear Charlie,

Okay, you and Cara and little Georgina are two days past your due date. In 1971, little Thea Claire or Aaron Riel would emerge fifteen days after the due date. I'm just sayin'. Like you, I was interested in a world of things, but a cervix was my principal subject of thought.

However, a number of other things was going on. I was on a Canada Council year, taking a break from my job in Montreal, living in a commune with old and new friends, and being a young writer who already thought of himself as a veteran. So, the day before Thea or Aaron's assigned birthdate, the chest of drawers ordered by my mother from Eaton's arrived after lots of mix-ups and delays. A friend brought around some premium hash, a lovely knitted shawl or blanket for decorating the baby, and the latest version of his manuscript for my tender editor's eye. Lionel Kearns phoned and told us that the latest meeting of the English department at Simon Fraser University indicated that I probably had a job there. Copies of my new book of poems *Touch* arrived at last. I thought: if the book can arrive, so can the kid, eh? Oh, and bpNichol's new book arrived in the mail. Deliveries were mostly pretty good in those days. After checking the mail, and noting that it was not my day for cooking nor was it Angela's, we went out to buy lots more baby stuff, this large woman and I.

Wait! What is this about the "next ten to eighteen years"? Are we supposed to take that long to get this book of intellectual letters done? In eighteen years, I will be—uh, old. Regarding your question about how I did all that stuff while being a dad: you don't know, nor will you find out, the half of it. Let me just say that I did a lot more than write and teach and be a dad.

By the way, you did not say anything about what interesting cravings Cara had. What did you have to go out in the middle of the night and get? Angela, who was a hamburger addict, simply became a hall-of-fame hamburger eater. Now, this was 1971. This was before there were chain burger joints on every corner, and before the idea of the twenty-four-hour fast food joint had become a part of the cityscape. I had to drive miles in an unreliable Chevrolet some nights.

Ah, a "self-conscious awareness of living in personal history." I remember that ("I" being an old guy who writes a lot of things that start, "I remember") very well. The air around you is *meaning-ful*. I think the therapists and insurance salesmen call such times "life-changing events." It's life-changing with music. You put on your right shoe, and you feel, *Here I am putting on my right shoe just short-ly before my daughter is born. Here I am jumping out of a DC3 with a parachute on my back. The air makes a sound as I walk through it.*

Now to the part of your letter that is about music. I wasn't a trumpet player, though my brother Roger was. I, with my buddy Willy, was a tuba player, a double-B-flat tuba and sousaphone player. I crashed into things going through doors. But the double-B-flat tuba has the same fingering as a trumpet, so when I was in the air force I bought a trumpet off a guy. I was always buying things off guys who could not wait till payday. I kept that trumpet for four decades, hoping that I would one day be a sudden virtuoso. Then a little girl, maybe seven years old, was visiting with her mother. She picked up the trumpet and just started *playing* it. I gave it to her.

Lou Reed? One day in 1968, I got a call from Gerard Malanga, a poet I knew who used to wear leather and carry a whip around Andy Warhol's Factory. That's where the Velvet Underground was the house band and part of the Exploding Plastic Inevitable. Gerard said I should come down and make noises behind Nico that would live for all time on tape. I was tempted, as I often was by this kind of stuff, but I decided to stay and be famous in Canada. I said to Gerard, as I often did in these situations, "Gerard, I'm just a simple country boy."

Your guide through the ineffable,
GB

December 30, 2013

Dear Simple Country Boy,

Well, this is somewhat embarrassing after all the drama and talk of "personal history" in my last letter. The little one must have gotten word that the Occupy movement had inspired a bit of optimism in her father, as she's turned Cara's womb into her own little Zuccotti Park and is refusing to leave. Today's eight days past the due date, taking us into week forty-two of Occupy Cara. To paraphrase the movement, it appears that one cannot evict a baby whose time has come.

As the due date came and went, leading into the most anticlimactic Christmas of my whole life (including the winter when I was fifteen and had to work at the A&W at the mall on Boxing Day), the weird feeling of imminence gave way to a sort of punchy, snippy anxiety. (I got into two slightly above-minor arguments with my brother and a couple of cousins, both pre- and post-turkey. Even the famous tryptophan didn't take the edge off.)

Then a strange thing happened: the adrenaline and anxiety, which were not sustainable over the long term, gave over into a feeling of non-reality. I often feel like turning to Cara and saying, "Remember that time when we were going to have a kid?" Although I know, intellectually, that she's coming, it's no longer with the same visceral certainty that she's right around the corner that I had on the due date. (By the way, Jesus, did I ever feel stupid for shovelling that snow. By the time every last bit of it had melted, my back was still killing me, and the kiddo was nowhere in sight.) Yesterday was the final performance of the play I wrote, and in the program I'd put a little shout-out to my baby girl, who, I said, would be born at some time during the run. Man plans, God laughs, baby stays curled up in her warm little womb.

Today we met the doctor who'll be delivering the baby, since

Dr Wong left on Boxing Day for Disney World with his family. The backup doctor is a very sweet, odd old guy who was wearing what appeared to be either a leisure suit or a polyester Maoist jacket-and-pants combo underneath his lab coat, the pockets full of folded forms and charts pertaining to other patients. His receptionist gave Cara a Styrofoam cup for her urine sample. He asked us if we believed in prayer. All in all, it was a very strange afternoon.

When we got home, I was filled with a manic comic energy and took to social media to rattle off old-school, roast-style one-liners about my baby girl. "I'm not saying my daughter's late, but she's already babysitting other kids." "I'm not saying my daughter's late, but she's already embarrassed she used to like One Direction and Justin Trudeau." "I'm not saying my daughter's late, but she just told us she wants to 'take a trimester off to find herself.'" I also pointed out that, after having listened for nine months to how unfair it was going to be for us to have her on Christmas, now we had to worry about her sharing her big day with Ukrainian Christmas.

Everyone's full of advice, but we've been doing everything we're supposed to. We've been walking so much, I've lost two-and-a-half pounds since Christmas. Cara's been guzzling raspberry leaf tea. We've even gone all the way a couple of times. Then, of course, there are those who insist that she'll "come out when she's ready" (though, as Cara points out, if that were the case, hospitals wouldn't need incubators). All we really want is for people to say, "Yeah, it must suck. Your eager anticipation is profoundly understandable."

I've actually resolved that once I'm a dad, except in cases where I am asked for specific information, I will simply echo back to expectant parents whatever they're giving me. If they're excited, I'll share their excitement; if they're down about something, I'll tell them I get it. People keep offering information, but really, all we're looking for is empathy. Although I think maybe it's their way of empathizing.

Both "Thea Claire" and "Aaron Riel" are great names. Our name for a boy was (and in future, may still be) "Rémy"—I'll save our non-Georgina girl's name for the letter announcing her arrival. I was going to be called "Catherine" if I'd been a girl, though as a joke my mom used to tell people that the girl's name they'd chosen was "Shi-teen." What would you have been named if things had gone the other way, Y-chromosome wise?

Love,

Shiteen

P.S.: I just realized I wrote that whole letter without addressing the fact that you almost noisily backed-up the Velvet Underground. I guess that serves as some indication of how myopic, solipsistic, and single-minded this obsessive waiting has made me.

Dear *Carlos el asiduo,*

Was your mother by any chance of the Shuswap persuasion? I ask because among the BC Interior Salishan-speaking peoples there is a supernatural creature named Sh-teen who's sort of a devil or a scary Loki or *duende* figure, if you are looking at the *duende* that scares the horses at night. There is a short discussion of Sh-teen on pp. 81–2 of my novel *Shoot!* Well, there is a character named Charlie in that book, too.

Come on, you mentioned your Panto. I know that this book is about our daughters, but product placement has its uses.

I think that my mother once told me what my name would have been if I were a girl, but I can't remember. I do know that I was supposed to be Richard, and they chickened out at the last minute. My parents finally named my youngest sibling Richard but immediately started calling him Jim. When I was a teenager, I planned to change my name to Theodore. I don't think that had anything to do with naming our daughter Thea. She was kind of named after Althea Gibson.

This Thea person was a little like your Georgie girl, taking her time about any debut. I think I mentioned that she was first scheduled for September 22. By September 29, Angela's cervix was open to the size of a twenty-five-cent piece, and Dr Herstein said that her due date was October 4, which was to be the date of our last birth class. How dramatic and educational it would be, we thought, if Thea arrived at St. David's Church in West Vancouver in the middle of a birth class. During these days, the kid kept moving, partly from side to side, but all the while down. On October 2, I listened to her heart, which was fast and strong and loud. I don't think she was getting all that much sleep, what with the tossing and turning in there. "The pelvic floor," I whispered at Angela's belly. "Head for the pelvic floor."

I am intrigued by the doctor in the disco duds. Is he for sure going to be the delivery man? That is, when is Dr Wong due back from Disney World? I think that if this is a narrative we are attending, you should develop the backup doctor as a character. For example, could we have him always carrying a Rex Stout mystery with him? I always wondered whether Luke Short was a pen name for Rex Stout. (For those people who are marginally older than Charlie and Cara's kid, you can Google those names.)

I often think of you fussing and fretting and pacing and taking a trip on desperate brain medicine, Charles, and I sympathize. I know that you are likely giving Cara lower back rubs, and I say that you could use one yourself. You are my hero, and Cara is my heroine, and this is my favourite story right now. Better than HBO, with a much more interesting O.

Speaking of which, what are your dreams like? I dream a lot anyway, and a lot more when I am travelling, and I hardly ever analyze the dreams. Around the time of Angela and Thea's due date, I dreamed a lot. In one I dreamed that I found our two famous Chihuahuas Frank and Small in the refrigerator but checked and saw that they were still in their box. In another the baby was born with its navel in its forearm. A nurse said that that is not the usual situation. In another, I was involved in an old-time gun chase. Some dissident general was on a roof firing a bazooka, and despite our officer's distrust, I took his extra rifle and joined in the fight, etc. I mean, really, dreams are like television that you are too young to understand. Or Language poets.

You're hearing from an older guy who still has trouble understanding the waking state. Here's my advice: write a lot of books, then to thine own shelf be true.

Love—
Theodore

Dear Daddy Charles,

I know that you have been (a) rather too busy to write me and this book a letter—an excuse I don't accept, your being an energetic and young man—or (b) piling up the experience that will take you pages and pages to report. So I just got tired of waiting and decided to tell you what I told my diary starting Thursday, October 7, 1971. I notice that in the diary I wrote "September" and had to correct it, perhaps sub-thinking of the kid's original due date.

Some of this stuff forms a part of a story I wrote a while later. It is in a volume (because we try to mention our books and shows as often as we can) titled *The Rain Barrel.*

Thea was finally born last night at 10:36. Angela went into slightly induced labour at ten-thirty in the morning, having been in the Willow Pavilion of Vancouver General Hospital since Monday afternoon. At twelve-thirty, I arrived, and we went into our drill, but the contractions were quickly sharp, and Angela was going into stage C very early, and sometimes could not stay on top. This because she wasn't dilated enough, and the baby was posterior. Angela was having what head nurse Davidson called uncoordinated contractions. She had Seconal at five-thirty, and I came home. But I was called back at six-forty-five because she wasn't sleeping. She had a local in her cervix, and that did it; she felt a pushing urge and this called for rapid panting, and as nurse Davidson and I massaged her you could see the baby turn around, opening the cervix. Pretty soon Angela was wheeled into the room across the hall.

(By Friday evening, I felt as if the kid was more than her forty-seven hours old, because I had been up to the Willow Pavilion so often. In the wee hours of the morning on Thursday, I had sat in the dark in our quiet rented Kitsilano house and emptied a big glass of Canadian whiskey. I never used to drink Canadian whiskey.)

Earlier, while pushing on Angela's tailbone during contractions, I could feel the baby's head. From the time that baby got turned around the right way, things went much faster and Angela was more in control. She opened from 3.5 cm to 8 cm in little over an hour. So we were in the delivery room, and I didn't know that was anything more than just the place for that local injection. Anyway, the team was in and out for the first hour as Angela went through transition: Dr Archie Herstein, head nurse Davidson, who always told Angela what the situation was, and several young nurses. Finally the doctor put his fingers in and let Angela push slightly, and I in my green hospital garb and ridiculously small cloth hat and mask with big eyeglasses over all could hear the lip go over with a gentle and insistent sound.

Then Angela started pushing, her face going beet red in her determination, and I was as busy as can be, giving her moisture for her lips and lifting. Angela was doing the breathe and block, and I was holding up her head from the right side, Davidson and another nurse pulling on her arms hooked under her knees, what simple power and leverage of the human body, no stirrups or wrist straps, another nurse looking at the clock and listening to the baby's heart—150, 160, 160. Davidson said the highest pulse was because the baby's head was now between vertebrae. Angela thinks this is going on a terribly long time.

Doctor Herstein and others went out for a smoke, and the young nurses urged and cheered, looking at Angela's groin during her determined pushing. We persuade her that she is making fine progress, though Davidson, always truthful, says the baby is slipping back quite a bit. Dr Herstein looks like a painter on his stool, stopping to reflect over the canvas between contractions. He gets the long needle and gives Angela the two local shots up there. Testing her, he taps and she says it feels the same. A nurse suggests an epidural and Dr Herstein says nope, she wants to do it all.

I move around to do the pushing from the head end of the table (and you will notice that the tense keeps shifting here—how could it be otherwise?) and from here (same for point of view) I have a perfect view of the mirror, though now I can't see Angela's face up close as well. From here I watch the episiotomy, turning away after a while, but I watch Herstein working like a sculptor now, and there is bright red blood flowing down like a miniature Montmorency Falls, and the soapy stuff laid on liberally. During the next pushes I can see not only the slit of grey hairy head, but now the whole pelvic floor bulging with the shape of the little head, and everyone is cheering like mad now.

Herstein asks Angela whether he can use the forceps (which he has sent out for, and they are slow in coming) to hold but not pull. She says okay, because on the previous contraction he said he couldn't really get control of the head. (Here I was now thinking it was a boy.) On the next one he is holding the forceps with one hand, elbows up, cotton swabs in Angela's doorway.

Now Angela has to block and push five times instead of the usual two or three, and the dear woman pushes, working harder than ever before in her life. Half-way through, the nurse on the right pokes in the pit, and I look back to see that tiny head coming out between the two big spoons, which are then dropped. Now the head is out and Angela remembers perfectly to go into her pant. I see the bones moving in the head, rippling, and before we know it, out comes the body, beautiful shape hanging purple from Herstein's hand, thick twisty soft cord dangling, I think for a microsecond that it's a boy, but everyone says it's a girl, I see, Angela sits up to see and cries, "Oh, Baby. Oh hello, Baby!" and this is the most emotional moment in my life, I've got love blazing out of all my senses, to Angela and Thea, now I remember, I was laughing, laughing, with love. There, I said it.

I watch the cord being cut, but before that, immediately on coming out, she made a little cry. But before that, the most beautiful thing, her little head, amazingly little head, turned by itself, to Angela's left thigh. Angela had just pushed her out!

(A while before, when the doctor was in position, he and a nurse moved the big light into position and turned it on, so Angela could see her pelvic floor better in the mirror. Such gestures are to be appreciated.)

So here was the baby, out, and she is moved over to her crib, and Angela is all smiles. I'm noticing that Thea has really big hands, light hair, and nose, ears, chin, like Angela's. She is still purple quite a while later, and I'm wondering how long before she turns pink. I'd been under the impression that it would happen in a minute or two. The last things to remain purple were her feet. Now Herstein is doing a lot of stitching. It takes more than half an hour, Angela starts cursing him: "Ouch! You're hurting me, you bastard!" She says a word less polite than bastard. He's heard it all before.

Everyone says she is a beautiful baby. Thea lies there with her eyes wide open all the time, and often I see her whole chin trembling. Shock, I suppose. They are slooshing her and putting drops in her eyes, and listening to her heart some more.

"Oh, wow!" was my summing up.

Yours,
The Wise Patriarch

January 13, 2014

Dear Patriarch,

You are correct in pointing out that I am long overdue for a letter—and the fact is that, even now, having put it (and so much else) off for as long as I've been able to, I'd still give just about anything to keeping putting this (and everything else) off indefinitely. I'm not doing that, though, because 1) it'd be rude and inconsiderate to you, my pal and co-author, and 2) I figure I ought to get these memories down now before they're gone, as they are already receding across the most expansive fortnight of my life so far.

Incidentally, I was moved by your last letter and recognized many of the details, even if they were different from ours; I, for instance, didn't see then look away from an episiotomy, but I could hear it, and winced—a kind of nightmare butcher-counter sound I wouldn't mind unhearing. But, to employ a cliché (and who doesn't when it comes to kids?), I'm getting ahead of myself.

On New Year's Eve, Cara and I went into the hospital, Burnaby General, for something called a Non-Stress Test to make sure that everything was okay with baby and to see if we wanted to get an induction. The nurse who saw us was named Rhoda—a very thin, short-haired Chinese woman who gesticulated emphatically whenever the subject was any kind of vaginal insertion. Rhoda was confident and without nonsense and impatient of doulas, and pointed out to Cara that she was having contractions that she, Cara, seemed not to be able to feel. We went downstairs for an ultrasound to make sure that there was still enough amniotic fluid for a comfortable stay, as well as to make sure that the placenta and umbilical cord were still in fairly good working order. Everything was good, except that the room in which we had the ultrasound was so bizarrely and cacophonously lit—neon, lamp light, monitors, and huge patches of darkness—that Cara and I each began to see wavy, rainbow lines in our vision, and I started to worry that I was having a stroke. We had been told by our backup doctor, Dr Hii, that an ultrasound this late would be anticlimactic, as the baby is too big to see clearly—like standing, he said, two inches from the Mona Lisa. He was right.

Leaving the ultrasound, we headed back upstairs having made up our minds to begin induction the next day, January 1. The first step would be to insert a catheter into Cara's vagina, inflating a balloon full of water behind the cervix. I believe this is to put the child into a more festive atmosphere, giving their arrival a sense of occasion. We were told to come back early the following morning.

We had planned, if we didn't already have a kid by New Year's Eve, to go to the Laugh Gallery stand-up show at the Cambrian Hall, hosted by our good friend Graham Clark, and I would drop in and do a spot. But we opted instead for a quiet night for the two of us, excluding even Cara's mom, who had arrived in town on December 17, thinking she'd be in just in time for the birth. Walking around Trout Lake, we phoned Dr Hii on his cellphone, letting him know our decision. "I know," he said, sounding almost impatient. "Your wife needs to trust me." We had no idea what he meant, and began to wonder what sort of hands we'd been left in by Dr Wong. (Let me deflate this little bit of suspense: within a few days, we loved him.)

Cara and I were convinced (as it turns out, wrongly) that since we'd be starting induction the next day, this was our final night without child. In bed, we started to fool around lightly, giggling, when in the midst of kisses and gropings, we were simultaneously struck by the imminence of what was happening—not sex, of course, but the seismic change that we had deliberately brought about and that now hung over us. As happy and excited as we were, we were each seized by a kind of mournful nostalgia for the just-us-ness of our lives until then. We each started to cry, and the chuckling game of grab-ass became something a lot more serious, even solemn. It was probably the most intimate moment I've ever shared with anyone. I'd never felt closer to her.

January 1 was largely an anticlimax, and I can remember almost none of it, except that we met our nurse, Shirley, Rhoda's opposite number in build and temperament, Rubenesque and constantly giggling, though also of Chinese descent. She and a much-more-friendly-than-the-night-before Dr Hii gave Cara her balloon and we went home, scheduled to come in the next day, after the catheter had worked some of its cervix-stretching magic. They also gave Cara a pill to help her sleep despite the nerves and excitement; I don't remember if I took anything myself.

The next morning, we arrived packed with everything we were supposed to bring—baby clothes, mama clothes, toothbrushes, etc., along with granola, beef jerky, the complete *Larry Sanders Show* on DVD, books, and a laptop. We even got the fancy birthing suite that we'd seen on the tour of the hospital, the one with the window. Shirley hooked Cara to an IV full of oxytocin—and get this: Shirley's pet name for the IV stand is, no shit, either "Charlie" or "George," and since there was already a Charlie present, she called him George. The drip was slow; it went on for hours and hours. We watched *Larry Sanders*, called a friend to bring by more DVDs, basically lazing for most of the day. I went downstairs to the cafeteria to get a cup of tea and, taking the concrete stairs to get back to the birthing suite, fell and cracked my right knee right on the step. This, coupled with an unexplained pain in my left toes, meant that I was limping on both sides the whole time.

By the late afternoon, the flow of oxytocin had increased, as had the contractions, and it became difficult for Cara to concentrate on the DVD, so we turned it off and turned on the delivery playlist that I'd made for her in iTunes. In the middle of Otis Redding's "These Arms of Mine" (ninth song on the list), her water broke. The types of contractions brought on by synthetic oxytocin are much harsher and closer upon each other than those which occur naturally, and before long, Cara was in a great deal of pain. I knelt by her side to comfort her, momentarily forgetting my knee injury until I crashed down on it with the full weight of my body, then swallowed the excruciating pain. (In the middle of labour, I wasn't about to say to Cara, "Guess how much my knee hurts!?")

Pretty soon, Cara was in a dolorous trance, eyes rolling back and almost completely outside of herself. She was desperately huffing the laughing gas with each contraction, then was given fentanyl. Our plan had been that if Cara wanted an epidural, she would ask three times. We got there pretty quickly. Through the pain, she managed to keep stoically still so as not to sabotage her spinal injection; within ten minutes her pain was tolerable; in twenty, she was managing well; by forty, she was conversing politely through contractions of the same strength that had her doubled over an hour before. She was almost instantly herself again. We both came to the conclusion that epidurals are pretty fucking great (a fact driven home in relief later that night by the screams of a mother who, for reasons that remain unclear to me, wasn't able to get one in time).

Labour slipped back into a certain uneventfulness again after that, with Cara sort of dozing, and our dear Shirley ended her shift, to be replaced by our equally dear Angela—a tall, narrow-faced, dark-haired white nurse with massive eyes. As midnight approached, I was famished, unsatisfied with beef jerky and granola. I managed to call our pal Steven, who brought me some vegetarian food from a restaurant that was open late; I was as grateful to him as Cara was to the guy who gave her the epidural. Dr Hii arrived to see where things were at. Over the next few hours, Cara's reticent cervix finally got to a place where they wanted her to push. Like you, I had a position: my left hand behind her right shoulder, right hand in the crook of her knee.

Except that every time Cara pushed, the baby's heart rate plummeted, which is expected, except that hers was taking a longer time than normal to get back up. No one was certain what this meant—it could mean that the cord was too long and wrapped around her neck, or it could mean that it was too short. They also noticed what looked like meconium, meaning that the baby may have pooped already (a risk with post-mature babies), which potentially meant that she was breathing in the sticky, tar-like substance. Cara started to get nervous. I was scared meconium-less.

I am a catastrophic thinker by nature and nurture, George, so as we waited for the obstetrician to arrive, my mind went to some very dark places—places I didn't leave completely until long after the birth. Between us, Cara and I decided that we wanted an emergency C-section, but when Dr Gruntman, the obstetrician, arrived, the heart-rate issue had sort of resolved itself (it was no longer taking so long to come back up), and since he said the head was close, he could do a vacuum birth. We later found out that he would have been paid more money if he'd done the C-section, which made us feel pretty warmly toward him. I was once more asked if I wanted to cut the umbilical cord when the time came—I'd said no before and said no again. Both doctors' faces dismissed my abstention from the process, saying they'd revisit the question at the moment of truth. I could tell they thought I should cut it.

The vacuum, as I remember it, was shaped almost like a skullcap attached to a fishing line. Terrifyingly, it sucked right off and snapped back in Dr Gruntman's hands several times. The room had filled with nurses plus a pediatrician who, like Dr Gruntman, had been rousted from bed, and as Cara pushed and the fetal sport fishing progressed, I became convinced that we were not going to take a healthy, bouncing baby home with us. There was meconium, and something wrong with the cord, and the baby's hand was in an inconvenient position, and Dr Gruntman's vacuum line kept snapping back with a terrifying force. A deep, anxious foreboding overtook me, and I watched the heart rate monitor and listened to the episiotomy, all the while whispering loving words of encouragement into my wife's ear. When the baby's oddly coloured, lifeless face emerged from Cara's vagina, I couldn't bring myself to believe that she was okay. They offered to put the scissors in my hand to cut the (as it turned out, nearly half regular-length) umbilical cord, and I did it, and it was no big deal, in any sense of the phrase. I can't remember if they brought her to the warming/weighing station before or after they put her onto Cara's stomach and chest, but there was a cough that Nurse Angela was ecstatic to hear, but which I found unconvincing and figured she was trying to make us feel better. On Cara's chest, the baby's eyes and tongue moved so slowly, and she was so calm, that I was sure we'd only have her for a few minutes, even as a wave of love for her came over me.

Then the paediatrician ran his tests, and she was fine. I asked again and again, maybe five times that first hour, but like the colour slowly coming into your Thea's body, suddenly the confidence that we were going to have and get to keep a healthy, breathing little daughter seeped into me.

Joséphine Ji Quan Ng-Demers was born at 6:15 a.m., January 3, 2014.

Our girl shares her first name with not only her grandfather (my dad's middle name is Joseph), but with two of her great-great-great-grandmothers on the Quebecois side. Her Chinese name, Ji Quan—which was composed by her grandmother and means "jade person"—links her to her cousin Griffin (whose Chinese name is Ji Yu) and was chosen to honour the memory of my mom, Robin, because it sounds similar to the Cantonese word for that red-breasted bird, which is *ji gung liu*. My friend Veda Hille has suggested the diminutive nickname "Joji," which we have been employing to great effect. And although she has not been named after you, when I say "Joji" into my iPhone's voice dictation, it writes "Georgie."

We spent the first hour cooing and kissing over her a fair bit, and a new nurse (even Angela had now finished her twelve-hour shift) did some preliminary breast-milk training with Cara. My fibrous vegetarian food caught up with me at that point, and when my little brother and Cara's mother arrived to see the baby, I was on the shitter. Nevertheless, they were both delighted by their new little loved one; in a broken voice, very uncharacteristic of her, my mother-in-law said, "She's perfect," which, though somewhat trite, also happened to be true.

We moved downstairs then, with the help of a ludicrously sweet and wonderful British porter, to the maternity ward, where we would be staying in a private room (sandwiched between two others housing much louder babies than ours) for the next two days. Sleeplessly, we took in vital information about keeping our baby alive, watched as she was given a bath, etc. The days are smeared together now, though I know I slept through Dr Hii and Shirley's visits the next day. At one point, I remember lying on my bed, Joji on my chest, having given her my pinky finger to suckle. A little while after I had removed my pinky, she found she could put her own fingers in her mouth, and honest to God—less than forty-eight hours into her life—I had the feeling she was already growing up, figuring out she didn't need me.

There was a lot of sobbing those first few days—sometimes out of overwhelming, unalloyed love and joy, but just as often out of terror. I realized that when I held her, I felt one of two things for her, sometimes at once: either obliterating, transcendental love, or crippling, claustrophobic fear. For every time I looked at her with incredulous, buckled-knees affection, I would also ask myself: what have we done? We were in Heaven before, Cara and I. We had each other. We could do anything. What are we doing here? My anxiety disorders—especially my OCD, which involves repetitive, unwanted, intrusive thoughts, and has been largely under control for many years—kicked the doors in and made themselves at home.

The day we left the hospital was a brilliantly sunny one. I went to get the car from the long-term parking and said to the attendant, as a joke, "You may need to carry me back in there when I see the total." Her smile disappeared when she saw it—"Ooh … Why didn't you buy a week pass?" she asked, wincing. My heart sank. $200? $500? The short-term parking had been nearly fifteen dollars an hour, and we'd been at the hospital from Wednesday morning to Sunday afternoon. I braced myself. It was sixty-something. I laughed from relief.

We arrived home to a false-bottom normality—we had a nice FaceTime video chat with my dad and my stepfather in Halifax, before finding blood in Joji's diaper and losing our minds (we later found out this is normal with baby girls, and Dr Hii kindly saw us in his office, even though it was a Sunday afternoon). Joséphine was insatiable, suckling for hours at a go at the paltry colostrum that Cara was producing. We'd done a formula top-up in the hospital and once or twice at home. I became fairly good at changing diapers, remained terrible at swaddling. Cara's mom would come over for hours each day, making Chinese dishes that are part of traditional postpartum care called "The Month." The dishes work well on white guys, too, as it turns out.

The shift in mood away from primarily terror to primarily joy came in with Cara's milk. The French Revolution could not possibly have been as satisfying as the moment that full breast milk toppled the austere tyranny of colostrum at our place. Suddenly, Joséphine would get milk-drunk and sleepy, positively agreeable. Rather than seeming impossible, now things just seemed hard.

Which is not to say that the anxiety has bled out of the house. One of our first days back, half-awake, I was convinced that there was breathing coming from my pillow, and that the baby was stuck inside. Just this morning, Cara, while sleepily feeding the baby in our bed, looked over and noticed the empty bassinet and woke me, screaming, "Where's the baby?!" I have learned that a "shit storm," which I had heretofore considered a figurative expression, can be literal (I've been shat and pissed upon in something like a 3:1 ratio to what Cara has endured). The nights have been long—Joji prefers, in the wee hours, to sleep on somebody's (anybody's) chest rather than in her bassinet, and so most nights I've been up with her till about five or six, letting her sleep on my breastbone while I watch Netflix or read. Or sometimes I just look at her, watch her face move with sleep, scarcely able to believe how much I love her. And just as I was writing that, she began to fuss, and now I've scooped her back up onto me and my typing is slowing down.

Looking back over this letter, I worry that I'm giving pride of place to the terrified thoughts, the doubts, the panic. I hope it's also clear that I can already tell that along with marrying Cara, this is the best thing I've ever done. I can stare at this kid's face for hours, looking for me and Cara, sometimes finding us, sometimes just seeing her. I can't believe she's a little bit of everybody before me, and still someone completely new. She makes faces both beautiful and absolutely hilarious. Though I find fatherhood anxiety-making, daunting, and more than a bit claustrophobic, I'm very proud and excited to be a dad. And though we would have happily loved a funny-looking baby, I have never seen anybody so beautiful.

And even if sometimes it feels like babies were just a scam cooked up by the detergent industry (I've actually been thinking of charging seventy-five cents to see the baby, just to bring laundry quarters into the house), I will always take comfort in what my friend Seán Cullen told me: "Now that you're a father, you're the second-most-important person in two people's lives."

Love,
Joséphine's Dad

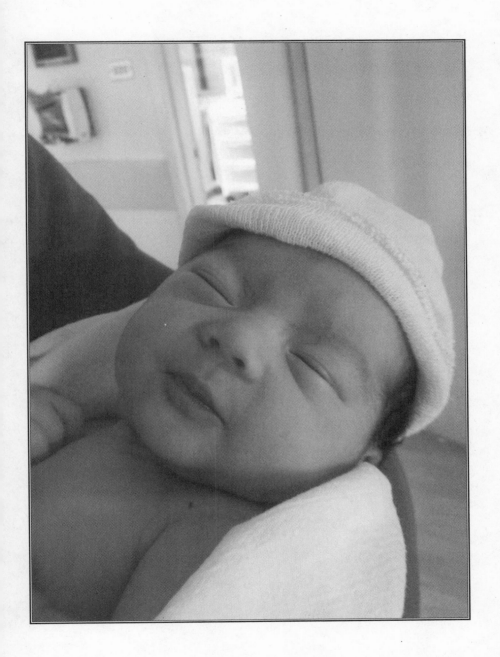

Chicxulub, Yucatán

As they say here, what's up, Niño?

Your heart-cooking picture of your dads holding and smiling at baby Joji put me in mind of a photo I have and which I turn to often. My parents had come down from the South Okanagan to stay with us in the ex-commune at 2249 York Avenue, around the time that we brought the baby home, and I have that nice unposed pic of my dad I told you about, reclining on the rotating bamboo chair I bought in Montreal, holding the tyke in almost the way your kid's grandfather would hold yours. Keep your photo forever, Charlie, even in this age of the easy snapshot. You will turn to look at the new and the old often. And then maybe when and if you ever get loose of this coiling mortality, your daughter will keep it to look at from time to time.

That's what I am hoping for.

And who knows? Maybe some of these pictures will make it into this book. By the way, I have a tentative title for the book. How about *George: the Dad*?

Anyway, you arranged to have a near-perfect baby girl by arranging to share her with a perfect woman. You wouldn't want to change that. That's why you named the kid after me instead of something red. But wait: isn't part of her name something to do with a robin? I think I will just bob away from that one.

And right back to say that I was pleased as punch to have Cara's IV named after me. Which reminds me, today is my sister's birthday, and this is true: she always used to call me a drip.

I hope you will forgive me if I tell you that the funniest part of your last letter was the part in which you cracked your knee and felt that it would not be a good idea to complain about the pain while your wife was experiencing what doctors and nurses always call "discomfort." I am impressed with your ability (read obsession) to bring humour to all situations. My buddy Willy and I have had a term for that since we were eleven: "Jokes to the end." Especially when it's Will that gets a nail in his foot, for example.

Angela and little Gumpy (she got that name because when she was born she did not really have a neck, any more than Gump Worsley did. I met the ex-goalie a few years later and told him that we had named our daughter after him. "Oh yeah?" he replied. The same phrase was used by Doris Lessing when we were in a taxi to the Perth airport and I pointed out the road to the baseball stadium) didn't get to come home for about a week, because the thread that Dr Hertzman used to stitch up the episiotomy was infected, and the poor little baby had to spend her first week in a glass box because she was getting her first meals from infected milk. It turned out that the thread was surplus material from the Vietnam war, just another reason to oppose that USAmerican adventure.

"Hell, no! We won't go!" were her first words.

Anyway, Chuck, I really liked your birth report. I understand why we had to wait for it. But it felt like being there.

I dig what you are saying about being a catastrophist by nature. After we brought Gumpy home, I was always tiptoeing over to her little bed to listen for breathing. Wise people were always telling us that babies are tough, but I didn't believe it. Bulldogs are tough. Cuban infantrymen are tough. My mother's roast beef was tough.

Babies are more like fathers' hearts—sweet and tender and loud.

Yours from my Yukatán work table—
GB

January 31, 2014 (Chinese New Year, Wooden Horse)

Dear George,

The beauty of the closing line of your most recent letter has re-stored my faith in your literary instincts—a faith briefly cast into doubt by your title suggestion. My titular inclination is toward *Daughtering Old Men*, which would capture our love of both our girls and our puns.

Like you, I remain unconvinced of the toughness or sturdiness of babies. In a moment of overconfidence on the evening of Joséphine's two-week birthday, I decided to clip her fingernails with a baby-sized pair of clippers. I wouldn't be telling you about this, of course, if it'd gone well. Things went smoothly from left pinky to index as she snoozed and I snipped, but on her tiny little thumb my motor skills failed me, and a skin-breaking pinch roused her first ever pain-induced tears. (Even in the hospital, she had surprised the nurse by taking a shot with nothing but a whimper.) As you can imagine, having so injured my still-very-little one—having been not the one who offers comfort and solace in the wake of pain, but the one who introduces it—I felt like a great big bag of the stuff we spend most days wiping off the bottom of her.

My guilt swelled with the thought that, in addition to having marred her sweet little digit, I may have exposed her to some sort of tetanus or gangrene or some other deadly, nail clipper-hosted threat. I phoned a pal who has a two-year-old to ask him what he thought; he said it was probably nothing, but that I could call the nurses' ho-tline, 8-1-1, if it'd make me feel better. Now, in my own battle against hypochondria (which is these days known as "health anxiety," which robs it of some of it's neurotically romantic connotations), I'd long ago promised my psychologist to stop calling 8-1-1. But this wasn't for me (except that it pretty much was). The nurse told me to keep an eye on Joji, go to the emergency room if we saw pus, red streaks, or felt a fever, and that regardless, we should see a doctor the next day. In the morning. It was already fairly late in the evening, but I placed a panicked call to the man who has so far been the unexpected hero of my daughter's life, Dr Hii, who patiently agreed to see us first thing the next morning, before he had to teach Bible study. The next morning, he took a look at Joji's finger and said she looked fine, told us to keep an eye out for the same things the nurse had flagged, and gave us an ointment that he whipped up for us on the spot using essential oils—including, if I'm remembering properly, myrrh, which is an appropriate gift for a Bible study teacher to give to a baby who was due on Christmas.

The thing that kills me, as a worrier, is that you're actually supposed to worry about a newborn baby. All my life, people have soothed my anxieties by saying, "It's nothing. Don't even think about it." Now, the best I can get is, "Keep an eye on it. Take her to the emergency room if ..." (Incidentally, this past week I was reminded of the relative fragility of even the adult body when a wayward blackberry seed blocked a pore into or out of my salivary gland, causing a painful swelling and infection. Now I'm on antibiotics and have officially sworn off fruit in favour of cookies.)

I'm glad you liked the photo of Joji with her Papi (my dad) and Grandpapa (my stepdad Dwight), who flew into town from Halifax the Monday after the nail clipper incident. I'm a pretty big fan of it, too. I have nearly a week's worth of shots like it (though none quite as special as the one you've singled out). My hope is that years from now we can all just look at them fondly, as wonderful and carefree snapshots—but I have to admit that, in addition to great joy and a desire to capture precious moments, many of the photos were taken with a certain quiet fear and desperation.

My dad looks much, much better than he did when I wrote you my first letter; he's regained weight and hair, and recent tests show that he's responded incredibly well to his chemotherapy. So well, in fact, that his doctor has suggested that he move forward with a potentially curative stem-cell, bone-marrow transplant from his sister, my Tante Élyse, who is a perfect match for him. Over the next couple of months, he'll be broken down with more chemo to an immunological blank slate; parallel to his granddaughter, he will have an immune system built up by a string of vaccinations which he will receive as if for the first time. (Unlike his granddaughter, though, he won't have the valuable antibodies passed on through breast milk.)

This will be the second time in my life that one of my parents attempts to fight off a blood cancer by receiving a bone marrow transplant from one of my aunts. The last time, with my mother, ended the worst way that it could have. I only recently found out that graft versus host complications were part of what killed my mom. Now, the twenty-five years between that transplant and this one may as well be a century; the process is barely recognizable. Dad is an otherwise very healthy man and is optimistic about his treatment, and I am doing my best to share that optimism. I'd like there to be pictures of him and Joséphine for twenty or thirty years to come. But on the small, terrible chance that this was the first of only a few visits, I wanted to overcompensate. She will never want for images of herself wedged into the crook of her grandfather's arm.

They seemed to be mutually smitten with each other, Dad greedily and jealously holding her to himself, she looking up at him for what seemed like hours at a time. Earlier tonight, he spoke to her over the phone, and she pushed her ear into the receiver, listening keenly. Cara and I nearly collapsed in laughter at how endearing it was. He ate soup at the Argo Café while he held her. He ate sushi on Davie Street while he held her. He sat with her in the library at Mount Pleasant and read a book to her in French. I've got it all on my phone.

To shift gears ever so slightly: a quick note on farting. While we were in the hospital fretting about our daughter's general disinclination to burping, one of the nurses matter-of-factly assured us that, "Some babies burp, some babies fart." We have, on our hands, an advanced and prodigious member of the latter group. At one point, a few days ago, Cara turned to me and said, "Why do they sound like such adult farts?" Later in the week, she was holding Joji while sitting next to Dwight, when the former let out a big one. Cara could tell, by Dwight's respectful silence, that he thought it had been she who'd farted.

Cara, incidentally, is having a hard time thinking of herself as a mom, which is an interesting problem to have when you're spending twenty hours a day dispensing breast milk. When we were filling out the online form for the birth certificate, Cara tried to answer "Mother's place of birth" with "Hong Kong"; a few days later, when a friend asked, "And how's Mom?" she replied, to his confusion, "Good, I think she's happy to be back in her condo." Cara's working very hard, but we've both had to admit that, so far, parenthood has been much easier than we'd anticipated. Now, partly that's because we'd expected it to be really, really tough. It's also partly because we've only barely gotten started. But I've been getting somewhere between six and eight hours of sleep a night since the end of the first week. We try to keep pretty quiet about that around other parents.

As to your letter: I'll admit to an obsession with trying to make things funny. I come by it honestly; I got it from my mom, who referred to me as a "little comedian" as early as two weeks into my life, in her baby journal. Mom was hilarious, and I think it was very important to her that I would be too. I have to admit—sometimes I wonder what it'd be like if Joji turns out not to be funny, a comedian's version of that mawkish Richard Dreyfuss movie about the music teacher with the deaf son. But now and again she'll crack an asymmetrical smirk just like her father's, and I rest a bit easier.

Which is not to say that there's no room for seriousness. My Uncle Phil, Mom's little brother—who is also a joker—wrote and recorded a beautiful, earnest song for Joséphine, employing his sister's name as a metaphor to celebrate the shoots of new life in a family that's been through a great deal of heartache: "Just when it felt like tomorrow was a bridge already burned / The springtime came around and a robin returned."

Love,

Charlie, son of Robin and Daniel; father of Joséphine; pen pal of George

Yucatán, Groundhog Day, 2014.

Carlos el caro y Cara la querida;

I'll start this missile here on the south coast of the Gulf of México and probably finish it in West Point Grey, Vancouver, United Airlines willing.

I have just spent a long time looking through your last letter for the word "four" because last night as I was going to bed under a flotilla of mosquitos, I thought of starting a letter to you by using your expression "four-week birthday." Turns out that you did not write that in your letter, so I wasted all that time reading your letter over and over. I hope that our readers have such good fortune. So you must have written the phrase during your profligate social media hours. I have to say that as an old coot, I am glad to see this kid of ours being a protagonist of a book and not just e-mailed, tweeted, facebooked, dropkicked, googled, and linked in. Anyway, I was going to say: four weeks old. Four weeks old. Those are magic words. Knowing this, I said them five times. Sure enough, when I opened my eyes, there was a big slab of butter on the table beside my computer. I decided to spread the joy.

Now it is no longer Groundhog Day, and we are in below-zero Vancouver—little blighter must have seen his shadow.

So I've checked my diary for the time when little Thea was four weeks old, and I see that I was pretty worried. At three weeks her birth certificate arrived in the mail, so she was official, a living human individual. Yet I was always on edge, worried about sudden crib death, which was in the news then. On that same day she got her first sponge (well really, cloth) bath, and she was not happy about it. She had an awful diaper rash that I hated to see and kept hoping would disappear. She would always cry when someone took her clothes off.

"Odd girl," I was still cheerful enough to quip.

Things were not helped by the fact that the troubles between me and Angela had not disappeared as I had hoped would happen after the baby was born. I don't want to get into that stuff, even though I know that it was an important factor in the story. Some things outside the house helped me retain a sense or perhaps illusion of sanity. My selected poems had been published by McClelland & Stewart, the main big-deal publisher in Toronto. There were poetry readings to deliver or listen to all over town. There was still the weekly Traditional Pub Night, after which I would come home and stare into my daughter's bassinet for an hour. I was playing for and coaching the Granville Grange Zephyrs in the newly organized Kozmik Baseball League. The great Toronto poet bpNichol came to town for a reading and dropped in for his audience with the Gump.

My diary for November 5, though: "Worried about Thea—she has been this week receiving medicine for a fungus condition in her mouth and got it around her little asshole. Now the fungus, at least externally, has been clearing up, partly due to her not wearing anything between her legs. But she has diarrhea, the mother's milk just coursing through her as water, every few minutes, thirty-plus diapers today. The Spock book calls the water stool a sign of a severe condition, and said get doctor or hospital. Angela phoned the pediatrician, who is not there, but his partner said put her on sugar water and stop the milk and call him tomorrow. I'm worried. Her one-month birthday tomorrow, the day the USAmericans are going to blow the bomb at Amchitka."

Yes, raising a baby during the Cold War.

The nuclear test at Amchitka was particularly worrisome because it was a notoriously unstable volcanic island in the Aleutian Island chain, and because it was way out west in that tectonic chain, closer to the USSR than to the heart of the USA. It was a typical provocation by one set of bully boys inside suits against another set of bully boys in less-well-fitting suits.

I suppose that I should be proud of the fact that my baby daughter was born just when Greenpeace was. The brave little ship left her home port on September 15, planning to sail right to the Rat Islands group where the Yanks had been blowing things up good since 1965, and was intercepted by the US Navy. They did not stop the largest bomb ever detonated by the Home of the Brave, but they certainly set off what Greenpeace's Bob Hunter called a "mind bomb," and woke a lot of people up. Amidst the newspaper and television furor, the Yanks decided to quit the tests, and let the island go back to being the wildlife sanctuary it had been declared early in the twentieth century.

The story isn't all rosy, especially for those First Nations people who have been getting cancer ever since.

Oh, Charles, I just can't give you more than an inkling of my mixed feelings at the time. Part of me saw Thea Claire's new life as a refutation of the death machine; part of me felt a continuum of fear that ran right from the spongy earth of an Aleutian island to the soft blanket my naked child was sleeping on.

Aw, she would go through a lot of my little panics over the next year or two, but now she is more than forty years old, living in Edmonton, and driving a car that I am not supervising. I am thinking of you today, on your first trip across this country since Joji's arrival, enjoying your customary blithe calm.

Your scarred old grandpappy,
George

February 10, 2014

Dear George,

I want first to thank you for establishing a convention that we can start a letter one day and finish it the next, because it's just after midnight in Vancouver, past three a.m. where I am, and I will likely punch out a paragraph or two on this first go.

I arrived in Ottawa a few hours ago, and though I ought to find myself at the centre of the Canadian universe—the Conservatives announced a budget earlier today, so in the hours before I arrived all eyes were focused here—I feel instead far-flung from where the action is. Cara sent me a photo of Joji in the hands of her Gong-Gong (Cantonese for maternal grandfather), giving him a wider smile than either of her parents has ever been able to elicit. That said, she did shoot me a little grin outside the airport as I pecked her with kisses before leaving her in a different time zone for the second time in her life, and the second occasion in a week. On a pre-takeoff phone call from the tarmac, I learned that there was a red spot on her back, for which an appointment with Dr Wong has been made for tomorrow morning. Hopefully nothing as worrying as the terrifying asshole-fungus and diarrhea combination that you and little Thea went through with the Soviets. Jesus, I can't imagine. Although I can, as I imagine most new parents could, relate to the crippling fear of SIDS and the constant checking on breathing and moving. For most of this week, sneaking over to make certain that she's breathing hasn't been an option.

The timeline's been thus: right now, it's Tuesday night/Wednesday morning, okay? Last Wednesday, at about six in the morning and on about two hours of sleep, I loaded myself into a taxi bound for the airport to be flung all the way to Moncton for something called the

Hubcap Comedy Festival. I don't know why it's named "Hubcap"; maybe because, when no one's looking, you're supposed to try to steal the show. Whatever the case, I'd signed on to do it after much foot-dragging, months before Joséphine was born, finally deciding with Cara that it'd be okay because a) Joji would be six weeks old by then, b) I'd probably be in the mood for a couple of nights of solid sleep in a hotel room, and because c) well, this is how I make a big part of my living, and I'd have to go back to work some time. What we didn't know was that a) the festival would come on the heels of my getting two big cheques, royalties for the Panto and an advance for a book of essays (which I really ought to actually be writing, incidentally, rather than working on spec with you here), so we'd be feeling if not cushy then at least not desperate for the work, b) the kid would be two weeks late, and so decidedly not six weeks old by the time the festival rolled around, and c) we'd been sleeping like angels alongside our relatively laid-back baby girl, and the first sleepless nights I'd face since leaving the hospital would be in Moncton.

I bawled and bawled on my way out of the house, but even before that, on the days leading up to my departure. I was dreading being away from my little girl, afraid she'd forget my smell or my sound or whatever it is. I packed children's books with me to read to her over the computer from my hotel room across the country. I've been telling a joke in my act about having wanted to name the baby Vancouver because she's half-white, half-Chinese, and we can't really afford her, but I was leaving her and the city she resembled behind to go thousands of kilometres away to a town that was much more like me: half-French, half-English, not in great shape. I arrived in Moncton at about two in the morning on Thursday, stayed and did shows on Thursday, Friday, and Saturday nights, then flew out without having had any sleep at six a.m. Sunday, arriving home to Vancouver in the early afternoon.

Does it make me a terrible father that it wasn't as difficult as I was expecting it to be? Because it wasn't. I mean, I missed her to bits and thought about her all the time—I went into a French-language bookstore to buy her baby books (and brought the kind of "look-there's-a-dog-on-its-hind-legs" joy to the Acadian staff that only a francophone from Vancouver can bring; meeting someone from the West Coast who can speak French is as rare and exotic as meeting someone from Saskatoon who speaks Uzbek, or anybody from Wyoming), and Cara sent me an unending string of photos and videos on my cellphone, which I mooned over appropriately. But it wasn't as heart-ripping as I'd expected it to be—I got through it okay, which I never thought I'd be able to. When I confessed to Cara that this made me feel guilty, she told me she was relieved; it made her feel less guilty for wishing that she could get away for a break.

We couldn't have done it, of course, if Cara's dad hadn't been in town from Hong Kong, and the Moncton pot was sweetened when my dad drove up for the afternoon, with his sister—my aunt and god-mother Élyse, whom we call Coco, and who is Dad's bone-marrow donor. And for all my tough talk, when Cara texted me after I'd just landed in Vancouver that they were just planning to swing by and pick me up at the airport, not come in to meet me, I threw the cell-phone text message equivalent of a tantrum. She relented and was waiting for me with Joji when I came out at Arrivals. I scooped the baby out of her car seat and into my arms, and immediately started to cry. One of the other comics, my friend Darcy, was touched and tried to get a photo, but I turned away and huddled over the baby. I regret not having let him take the picture, because I'd love to have archived the moment, but I can't express how vulnerable and private a moment it felt.

I choked up a little bit when they dropped me back at the airport today, maybe fifty hours after they'd picked me up, especially after the smile I'd gotten. According to Cara, the books say her smiles are genuine now, not gas or anything, but I feel like she's been smiling for real from the start. At the very least, on her one-month birthday, she was smiling—smiling and lifting her head up and holding it up. I felt so lucky to have been home when that happened; it could so easily have happened while I was in Moncton. So long as we can go the next day and a half without any milestones, I'll make it back from this CBC *Debaters* taping in Ottawa without having missed any great changes, either. Except chubbiness. If you leave the room for a pee, you'll miss her getting a little bit chubbier. She really is my baby girl.

Whaddaya know, I wrote it all in one go after all.

Love,
Charlie

Feb. 11 Post-script

Dear George—in writing that all in one go, I feel like I may have missed some stuff that hasn't been covered yet: Joji's first Chinese New Year dinner and her beautiful costume for it, her love of her uncle, my brother's, paintings, and the fact that she'll just sit and stare at them for minutes at a time. There'll be loose ends like that that I hope don't get totally lost because they don't fit the narrative thrust of a given letter. I'll try and send a little p.s. like this when I feel like I've missed anything.

Love,
C.

February 16, 2014

Dear Chas,

I have to say that I am not unmoved by your gestures of adulation by imitation. As a father, I too went on my first lone trip to bring culture to my nation six weeks after the birth of my little poop-producer. And while I did not wing so far away, I did not moan and pewl into my diary about my lonely state. It was the olden days, and I was a Protestant lad, so I doubt that I made moaning and pewling phone calls, either. And, you lucky young pup, I was practicing dadhood long before antisocial media or even cellphones. On top of that, I took the train.

Which meant that I had to get up at the crack of six on a late November morning to catch the PGE dayliner from North Vancouver to Prince George, a twelve-hour-and-then-some trip, if I remember aright. This after a couple nights of four-hour sleeps. Then, like the idiot I was in those days, I talked with my poet pal Barry McKinnon till three-thirty in the morning. It was then that I told him that if Thea had been a boy, her name would have been Aaron Riel Bowering. Not long after that, Barry phoned us and asked whether they could lay the name Riel on one of their kids. That's how poetry and roll-calls got started in the early seventies.

You have to remember that on the birth of my first kid, I was pretty well mature in all ways. It happened two months before my thirty-sixth birthday. As I understand it, you were a seldom-shaving thirty-three when your heir entered our world. Furthermore, when I got onto early-morning trains back in the pioneer days, it was for the purpose of delivering intellectual lectures and difficult poetry to college people eager to hear what was going down. I didn't get away with a few jokes about current events plus the kind of charm that makes the hearts of all those groupies race.

In Prince George, I regaled them at the College of New Caledonia, then stayed up talking with northern poets till two-thirty the next morning. Then I had to get up at seven to catch the train to Edmonton. It is *dark* up there on November 24. Yeah, as the joke goes, and *cold*. Well, you know that isn't the way the joke goes, but you know how the joke goes. By the time the train got to Jasper, where I had to wait for a connection, my hand had thawed out enough to write in my diary. I didn't write about Thea. I told you I was tough.

So no, it doesn't make you a terrible father that you didn't find it all that difficult to be separated from your new kid and newly refurbished life partner. You know that's what us breadwinners do. A man's gotta do what a man's gotta do. I always used to remember this when Angela told me, "You gotta load of diapers to wash."

And as for turning away for a private weep with your baby at the airport—well, you can't archive *every* moment. I remember that we were always taking pictures of our rug-rat, but you with your digital hoohaw take more pictures every day than our whole daycare did in a month. I can tell you, though: you are going to moon away a lot of hours gazing at those pictures four decades from now—however pictures will be looked at then.

Oh, and as for the difference between smiles and gas? I hope you have not got so sophisticated as to quit smiling when you let go with a good one.

I did phone home from Edmonton, some time after midnight on the 26th. But I almost forgot. It was a short tour, but I got good crowds in both wintry cities, and I had a lot of good long conversations with poets in both places. It was almost like being a writer instead of a dad. How odd to realize that the baby I was taking the train westward to see is now a writer in Edmonton, and that Doug and Sharon Barbour, who were among the group I spent such a nice time with there, are part of her crowd now.

The CN rail trip from Edmonton to Vancouver was a much more mixed blessing. It was the Grey Cup train, and it was full of the kind of western Canadians who enjoy getting drunk and watching football in bad weather. I must have had a premonition; I had splurged on a roomette (well, I was going to bill the Canada Council, I suppose, but in those days I used to haul a heavy suitcase twenty blocks instead of calling a cab, even if I was to be refunded). I locked myself inside that roomette at eight-thirty that night, and went to bed until seven-thirty in the morning. You might guess that a) I was trying to catch up on the sleep I had been missing for several nights, and b) this was a way to shorten the time till I got to see my little family again.

But a good part of the reason was that I was filled with disgust for my alleged fellow humankind. At least in the sleeper half of that long train, those people were, as I wrote in my diary, "drunk, obscene, racist, sexist, etc." After seven-thirty in the morning, the noise had ebbed to some snoring and half-hearted cursing, and I was the only conscious person in the dome car, enjoying my first railroad view of the Fraser Canyon. It was a surrounding beauty much larger than the ugliness I had been surrounded by all night.

The Grey Cup game? It was one of the worst of all time. Calgary beat Toronto 14 to 11 in the pouring rain at Empire Stadium.

Curmudgeonly (hey, MSWord didn't redline that word!) yrs,
GB

Dear George,

It was nice of you poets to share names way back when. From what I understand, it was a source of mild consternation for my grandmother when Robin—the name she'd chosen for and given to her first daughter and my only mom—was borrowed by Granny's best friend to be bestowed upon her daughter too. Now there were two red-headed little girls named Robin running around in one little circle (I mean social circle, though it's not impossible to imagine them running around in a literal one, either). At the time, Robin wasn't really the unisex name that it became—it skewed much more masculine. In fact, when I was growing up, because my dad pronounced his name, Daniel, in the French way (*dan-yell*), when I'd tell people my parents' names they'd assume I had a pop named Robin and a mom called Danielle. Probably why I'm so forward-thinking, gender-wise, I'll bet. That said, part of the consideration that went into "Joséphine" was about choosing a name that could go either way; it's very pretty and mellifluous if she's a girly-girl (what's these days called cisgendered) but has the building blocks of a great butch name if she's so inclined. Today a lady who sold Cara a shirt told her that Joséphine was a very calming name, and I have to agree with that, even if it hasn't worked on me.

A few nights ago, little Joji made her first trip to the emergency room—in fact, we almost broke her twice this week. My heart still hasn't quite settled into my chest.

The first incident—the one that sent us to the ER—started innocently enough. I had actually planned on staying up all night anyway, since it was the day before my dad's stem-cell, bone-marrow transplant, and I had missed the chance to phone him during the day; I figured I'd wait up until four or five a.m. and catch him at the break of Halifax morning, ahead of the procedure. At around two or two-thirty, I was holding baby Joji, who was doing her now-typical hour-before-sleep semi-fussing. I was lying on our bed, sitting her up with her head lolled back into the palm of my right hand, when suddenly she shot forward. I managed, with relative gentleness, to catch her face with the heel of my left palm. Gentle or no, in the subsequent minutes she developed a straight, just-slightly-more-than-faint red line running vertically above her left eye. On a whim, we called 8-1-1, the nurses' hotline, but I guess the phrase "red line" is an automatic go to jail, do not pass go, do not collect $200 for them, since it can be a sign of sepsis. So at about quarter to three, we set out for quiet little Mount St. Joseph Hospital in East Vancouver—a hospital so quiet, in fact, that its ER closes at eight p.m. A notice on the door directed us to St. Paul's downtown, a trip I made with growing disregard for speed limits and red lights. My conviction that this was just a light bruise, nothing more, was bleeding away.

The fawning of the triage/admitting nurses over our little girl removed some of my anxiety—though it was quickly replenished as the guy checking in next to us told the nurse, "I just got back from overseas, and I've got this rash ..." One of the nurses cooed over Joji and showed her a picture of her, the nurse's, grandchild. Another admitting nurse said to me, apropos of Joséphine, "I'd like to hold her, but ..." and I wasn't sure whether or not it behooved me to offer her up. I didn't.

The next nurse—who took the baby's temperature rectally and found it to be at a borderline-high 37.5—was equally gushing. I guess when an emergency room shift is punctuated by a visit from a super-cute baby who appears to be perfectly fine, it's a bit of a treat. For her part, Joji seemed to be having a blast, alert as all get-out. She took a great big dump that made enough of a mess that a bit of it got onto her feet during the changing. After not too long, we were visited by a kind and patient young doctor, also a father, who said that Joji was fine (by now the line had pretty much disappeared). We were sent home, leaving the hospital just after four a.m., which was relatively reasonable given that we'd arrived around three, plus it allowed for a nice phone call with my dad in his hospital room across the country as we drove home.

Even though we'd been reassured, I was left with a residual buzz of anxiety about Joji's health (as you and the reader know by now, this doesn't take much for me). But my panic turned nuclear a few days later, last night, again around two or three a.m., as I stood in our bedroom, watching Cara and the baby in a bout of angelic post-nursing sleep, when to my horror, Mommy briefly awoke just groggily enough to want to put something onto the nightstand but not to realize that she was rolling over onto our child. Even though I saw the whole thing, it took me a long second to process it; then I hissed at Cara that she was on top of the baby.

Although the kiddo was evidently unscathed—smiling and cooing as I gripped her, dripping tears, asking if she was okay—I went into a panic-attack tailspin. I wondered whether we ought to head back to the ER, whether bones or organs might have been broken or burst. Tellingly, I worried that her ribs might have snapped and pierced her little lungs (I say tellingly because this was how my mother died; the osteoporosis she'd gotten from her leukemia treatments had made her bones so brittle that a sneeze had turned her ribs into shards and opened a lung). I made Cara call her dad, who happens to be in town at the moment, to ask what we should do. I phoned and woke up a friend of ours who is a nurse (despite the fact that she's very deeply pregnant herself, I still let her husband roust her from sleep). I couldn't handle making the decision not to go the ER myself; I didn't want the ultimate responsibility for the choice. In the end, we didn't go. All day today, I've been driving Cara and myself crazy by asking constantly if the baby's okay, whether we made the right call.

I don't know how long it'll take for this paralyzing fear of her fragility or impermanence—the same fear I had in the first hour after she was born, that we wouldn't get to keep her for long—to go away. I'm not sure it ever will. It's a terrorizing conviction in my bones, left over from the way I lost her granny, the original Robin. I remain essentially convinced, I think, that the degree to which I love somebody is bound up with the degree to which they're likely to be taken away from me.

It is a scary amount of love, what you feel when you look into your kid's face. Scary for me, anyhow. Like those magic tricks where somebody lies down on a bed of nails and has something smashed on their chest with a sledge hammer or something, and it works because the pressure is distributed just so. The love is a crazy amount of pressure, but it's survivable—even wonderful—because it's distributed just so. I can handle this amount of love if I know the weight of it can be spread out over the rest of my life. But I've got the kind of mind, as you know, that obsesses over what happens if the pressure shifts a little bit and my chest gets caved in. It's not doing me any favours at the moment.

Anxiously yours,
C.

Dear Carlos,

I thought about your persistent panic this morning as I looked up from my ridiculously easy *New York Times* crossword and saw that the back yard seemed to have no Bernese Mountain Dog sniffing around in it. As I had done on earlier occasions, I shuffled to the porch, looked around the corner of the house, and saw this time that the side gate was open. It was the first time this had actually happened, so I went into action. That is, I shouted down the basement steps toward Jean's workroom, "Side gate open! Dog gone!" Then as Jean went hollering Mickey's name out front, I headed upstairs to get my clothes on. But by the time I'd got my robe and slippers off, I heard Jean saying "Good girl" quite loudly at the front door, so I figured that she was not praising a neighbour's kid who had picked up her candy wrapper, and calmly reacquired my work outfit and joined in the dog-patting.

So you see, I am no stranger to alarm.

If that neighbour girl had been there, her name would probably have been Harold or Morris. I say this because your comments about your mother's sobriquet reminded me that the girls are taking all our boy names. In places such as Australia, they have made a bargain: if a girl is to be named for that red-breasted bird, her name has to be spelled "Robyn." It is a compromise that I will have to accept. I knew about female Sydneys when I was a boy, but they were mainly British girls at boarding schools, and probably in fiction. I guess that the mothers who purloined our name D'Arcy have kind of compromised, too, by calling their daughters Darcy. Or is that lost apostrophe the fault of mothers who do not know how to spell "it's"?

But what is going to happen when they take all our names? The last male Shirley I remember is Shirley Povich, the onetime great *Washington Post* baseball columnist. I knew a few male Beverlys when I was a kid because there were a lot of Brits in the South Okanagan. But then along came Hollywood, where actresses set about grabbing boys' names and splashing them onto the screens, big and small. Why couldn't Rene Russo be satisfied with Renée? When they give a movie a title such as *There's Something About Mary*, whom do they get to play the role of the woman with the most female of female names? Cameron Diaz. Cameron Mitchell is probably rolling in his cowboy grave.

They already had Audrey; why did they have to take Aubrey, the eighteenth most popular girls' name in the US last year? The one that really pissed me off in recent years was Ashley or Ashleigh or Ashlea or whatever. I figure that it probably came from some trashy soap opera, as most of the rave names do these years. Well, my eldest niece's name is Charleen, which is a name I have never liked, but at least they didn't name her Charlie after her father.

Well, enough of the rant. Now down to serious stuff—I mean panicking fathers. You know, the ones who think that 37.5 is not normal body temperature for a baby. But who redeem themselves by describing the wee offspring's magnificent evacuation during a change at the hospital.

You can tell that I am putting off sharing my own new-dad experiences of terror. I will confess to two of them that took place early in the new world. In both cases we were living in a less than perfect house on Balaclava Street. Apparently, some owner before us tried to turn it into a duplex, got caught, and decided to dump it on some first-time buyers with stars in their eyes. The upstairs, which one could reach by one of the two front doors, had a bathroom, the spare bedroom, my study, and Gumpy's room, where she could sleep as she always did, crosswise at one end of her crib.

Angela was out somewhere—perhaps at school; I can't recall whether she was a student that year. I was downstairs because I had a visitor, a young woman named Susan who had been in one of my classes at Sir George Williams University in Montreal. Every once in a while I would go and cock an ear at the stairway, the way you do, and then come back and sip some more coffee and talk about old times that were not really old. Then, on one of my staircase visits, I thought I heard a strange sound. It was indescribable, but because I had never heard it before, it plunged fear into my heart. It was very loud, and I ran upstairs, falling as I went, stricken with mortality. The baby was asleep in her diaper, but breathing as loud as a Ford truck someone was trying to start.

Somewhere in all the reading we had done to get ready for Thea's arrival, there had been a note about sudden soaring body temperature and how dangerous it was. *Oh, Jesus, no, my baby is going to die*, I thought. I grabbed her and her blanket, handed her to Susan, and got into my old Chevrolet. Susan sat with the baby in her blanket, which of course was a stupid idea—I should have doused the baby with cold water. Then I had to take a hell of a chance making the left turn onto 10th Ave., when I should have taken a right turn and headed for the UBC hospital. I was not thinking—I was trying to keep my nerve system inside me. It was rush hour. I exceeded the speed limit along 12th Ave. when I could, but usually the traffic was stalled. I cut a few drivers off. I went onto the sidewalk a few times. I thought about being a man with no child.

We finally got her to Vancouver General Hospital emergency, where she was taken away somewhere to be put into the care of people who knew how to save babies if babies could be saved, and I phoned home over and over, until Angela was there, and told her to grab a taxi.

For years I suspected that she suspected that our daughter was in danger while I was fooling with a young woman, but maybe not, and not.

I might even have prayed, as I would twenty-seven years later when it was Angela in the hospital and the young woman was Thea, trying to comfort me and retain her own sanity.

I know anxiety, Charles. I worry about being too late to catch every plane I am supposed to catch, and I worry about that plane disappearing from the radar. I fret about odourless gases filling the house while we sleep. I hate the idea of my daughter driving a car along a two-lane highway through the Rockies. During my long teaching career I had a sore stomach at the beginning of every semester, even though students said I could teach the shit out of any text.

The second example took place when Thea had just turned one and could toddle a little. I taught her to toddle by holding a stick for her to hold on to, and eventually I let go of the stick. It worked. Now she walks around Edmonton with a hockey stick in high-sticking position.

This time it was I who got a phone call from VGH. I was, unfortunately, out at Simon Fraser University, normally a fifty-minute drive from Kitsilano where we lived, and probably forty-five minutes from the hospital. I had been employed out there for a year, and had learned a somewhat complicated driving path, one that avoided the Lougheed Highway because it was often too busy. But for some reason, in my panicky run from my office to the distant parking lot, I decided to take the four-laner because the speed limit was higher. Now, you want to talk about terror? Traffic on the highway was creeping, and unlike you, we did not have the miracle of the mobile telephone. I was as rude as I have ever been on that drive toward Vancouver, but I thought my heart might beat so fast that I'd black out at the wheel of a Chevrolet.

Angela was a woman who once joked that the undertakers should outfit her casket with a telephone. As a Baptist boy who had not quite been ethnic-cleansed, I treated the phone as something to be avoided, but if it becomes necessary to use it, that usage should last no longer than thirty seconds. Angela, on the other hand, thought that any phone call that came in under an hour was kind of abrupt. So for a great deal of the day she could be seen with a telephone in one hand and a long cigarette in the other. On this occasion, she had been polishing something in our little living room, using a bottle of one of those furniture polishes that claim on the front of their labels that they are lemon-scented, while on the back of those same labels that the product should be kept out of the reach of children. Another difference between us was that I was always walking around putting the lids or caps back on things such as toothpaste, mayonnaise, and furniture polish, while she thought, I have to surmise, that such anal-retentive behaviour was uneconomical. Anyway, this time she had placed the capless furniture polish on a low shelf near the item she was polishing, when the telephone rang. The baby, who had been bottle-fed for a while, drank the lemon stuff. After a while, her mother spied her and somehow got her to the hospital. From there she phoned me, and I cut the conversation really short so that I could bolt out the door, not stopping to grab my lecture notes.

Of course I made it to the hospital, though it took an hour of chest-collapsing fear. Thea had had her stomach pumped. I wished that they would do the same for me. I might even have prayed again. I think I said "God" more often than I said X-rated words on the way to the hospital. For a whole night I was not a young writer—I did not give any thought to writing about this some day.

Your serene father-figure—

GB

Dear George,

I'm shamefully late in writing you; even now, I only have time to do it because I'm in a café for a meeting that the other person forgot to show up to. I have an hour and a half, two hours, in which I have absolutely no responsibilities. It's like I've found a $100 bill on the sidewalk; Prime Minister Borden shooting me a kiss from underneath his moustache.

It's really a bad time to have stopped writing as often, because as we approach the three-month mark, the pace of change has risen steeply. The wobbliness, for instance, has all but gone out of any head-and-shoulder-lifting. She's big now, closing in on fourteen pounds, heavy enough that, at the end of the day, there's a physical fatigue from having carried her, alongside the mental one. Likes and dislikes are trading places regularly: our little daughter, who used to hate being changed and love being bathed, now kicks against the bathwater with her increasingly strong legs, before settling into it with a very stern look on her face. On the other hand, when you lay her down to be changed now, as soon as the first buttons on her onesie start to be undone, she gives a broad smile.

My favourite smile of the day, though, is the one she gives when she sees me (or her mom) for the first time in the morning. It takes a few seconds for her to figure out who it is that she's seeing before a slow, wide smile spreads out across the whole bottom half of her face. "Hey, *that* guy—I love that guy! Haven't seen him in ages." Once she's scooped up in your arms, she spends a few seconds socializing, like a bit of office chit-chat at 9:02 a.m., before she gets down to her task at hand: staring at everything in the room, as intently and for as long as she can. She does it dutifully. There's a gold-and-black Chinese fan on our wall that Cara's dad—Ji Quan's Gong-Gong—brought back from Hong Kong a few years back. She can stare at it for minutes on end, the way she used to look at my brother's paintings.

Now, when I write it all out like this, it sounds like an idyll. So why have I been not-so-slowly filling up with general misanthropy and impatience, dread, fear, panic, not to mention anti-anxiety meds, over the past days and maybe weeks? It certainly doesn't feel like it's her or the responsibility of caring for her that's causing it. But it may be that the room that she's taking up is pushing every other fucking thing in the universe into a smaller, sharper shard of my time that feels like it's sticking right into my chest.

Chris, another new father who also works at the University of BC, remarked yesterday how it feels incredible that somehow the world doesn't just stop around you. Think about you, on the Lougheed Highway, trying to get to your little poisoned baby—shouldn't all those other humps on the road have just pulled over, or better yet disappeared, and let a desperate dad get through? But of course they didn't, because they all had places to get to as well. Maybe some of them even had sick kids they were rushing to see. It's an unseemly solipsism that slowly takes over—and it's even more insidious than regular solipsism, because it feels altruistic. You can convince yourself that you're not making it all about you—you're making it all about your kid.

So I keep trying to do all the other stuff I'm supposed to be doing, but it all comes with either a big heap of resentment that I'm being made to do it or guilt that I'm not doing it properly. Resentment: pretty much any email or phone call I get. Guilt: I call my dad every day to see how he's doing, and usually it's from the car. I call from the car because it's the only place I can do it where I don't have to (get to) hold a baby. But I also call from the car so that I can do two things at once—which feels wrong and insensitive somehow, to think of checking in on my father recovering from a bone-marrow transfusion as one of two birds to be hit with a single stone.

New parenthood. There's an old joke about sex and pizza that goes, "Sex is like pizza: even when it's bad, it's still pretty good." I feel like there needs to be an equivalent for being a new parent—having an infant is like calculus: even when it's easy, it's still pretty hard. I don't know enough about calculus to know if that's an apt metaphor. But I know that Joséphine could not be an easier kid—she's affable, sleeps long and well, eats well, likes meeting and being held by other people, likes being out with us—and yet our new life with her is still more than a bit overwhelming. Like I said, it's not that she feels overwhelming; it's that suddenly the rest of it is.

It might be that life's just as hard as it always was, but that now, at night, rather than zoning out in front of the television for a few hours, then reading before bed, we spend that time holding her, walking her up and down the stairs the way she likes, singing her "*La Complainte du phoque en Alaska*," the classic song by Beau Dommages.

I love that time with her. But it is exhausting as phoque.

Love,
C.

Post-script March 28, 2014

After my not so rosy letter yesterday, I wanted to send this: last night, Joséphine was quite fussy before bed. And specifically, she was fussy for her dad. So at some point, between three and four in the morning, while Cara was reading, I took the baby into the other room, holding her over my shoulder, then cradling her, trying to figure out why she was sucking on my shirt if she wasn't in the mood for a feed. It occurred to me to do something I hadn't done in several weeks: give my hands a wash (well, okay, it hadn't been several weeks since I'd done that; I'm compulsive, remember?) and give her my upside-down pinky finger to suckle. Turns out that that, and a song sung in a lower register than Mom can serve up, was exactly what she needed. As her eyes fluttered shut, I was filled with a pride that I'm probably not a good enough writer to put into words without sounding saccharine and queasy-making. But, man, did it ever feel special to be the only person in the world who could comfort her in that moment. It made me feel like an adult; it made me want to live forever. So, what I'm saying is, it's not all anxious hand-wringing.

And here's a stray observation, more than tangentially related: it is an amazing thing to watch your baby sleeping on her mother's chest, and know that every feeling of comfort and safety she'll ever have for the rest of her life will essentially be a metaphor of the real, literal moment that you are seeing.

April 1, 2014, really

Mon cher Charles,

Five years before this baby business, I had stepped out of the Topkapi Palace in Istanbul and looked across the water at the edge of Asia. No one in my high school class had done that. Two years before that, I had stood on the top of the Temple of the Sun at Teotihuacan. No one in my family had ever been there. Four years back, I had had my first novel published by McClelland & Stewart, THE Canadian publisher. No one in my Creative Writing class had managed anything of the like.

Now I had impregnated my wife nine years after our wedding, and nine months and a bit later she had, as they say, delivered a girl baby, and I was walking around being a father. Like, a few billion guys had managed that, and a lot of them didn't even have a university degree, but here I was, feeling as if every molecule in my body had been changed, and the universe itself had sighed and turned over in bed.

So, what did you do to contribute to this miracle?

Well, see, I took my pants down, and …

You know what it's like, Chas. I remember the day after I lost my virginity, much later than did my peers, I walked around thinking, *woo, everything has changed, I am a different form of life*. But becoming a father was way beyond that. You know the way young people today say something is "amazing" or "awesome" if they like it quite a bit? Well, back when we really meant it when we said those words, we might have said those words.

It was 1971, though. You recall that when I saw my offspring, or should we say outslide, here is what I said: "Oh, wow!" That's what we said in 1971 when we were impressed.

I don't know whether you are supposed to do this, but I innocently hoped that this shared human being would make her mother and me get along the way one always hoped a couple would get along. But as I read my 1971–72 diary now, I see that I was getting yelled at a lot. And I see that the kid had conditions at both ends of her alimentary canal that got us very worried when we read the Dr Spock book. One day we went through thirty diapers and I made several trips to the laundromat on Fourth Avenue and got yelled at when I came back home to our craftsman-style home on York Street. And me without any anxiety meds. Well, Angela had lots of meds because she had been seeing her shrink for a decade. I had writing, but I had to do it in laundromats during the spin cycle.

It's not that I am wallowing in baby envy, Charles. That baby Thea was the best thing I had ever seen, better than all the jewelled rooms of the Topkapi Palace.

Her first winter was a very snowy one, but when she was just over two months old we got her and our two Chihuahuas Frank and Small into our old Chevrolet two-door and went over the Hope–Princeton Highway to my parents' place for a pre-Christmas visit. There we were like one big happy family. I stayed up late getting some writing chores done, and little Gumpy spent the days staring with her big round eyes at her aunt and uncles and grandparents and cousins and all the little dogs. I was learning how it was that proud papas get that way, and as Angela and I spent our ninth anniversary in the house I grew up in, I looked at my dad as if to say, See? I can do it after all.

It was so lucky that I was on my first Canada Council writer's grant that year. It meant that the number of jobs I had to do (while getting yelled at for lazing around) was almost manageable. One of the first things I had to do when we got back to snowy Vancouver was to read and grade 125 applications for Canada Council writer's grants. I waited till after midnight when wife and daughter were abed, and went through these on the kitchen table. According to the description of the grant we were living on, I was supposed to be writing a novel or something. Well, I was also running a magazine, trying to write at least four letters a day, writing book reviews, shopping, laundering, shovelling snow, cooking, washing—you know, all that stuff you do in your spare time. Thank goodness I wasn't a janitor for a whole apartment block as I was when I had my first teaching job at the University of Calgary.

But here's what kept me going, and I am so pleased to see it happening in your letter. "The baby Gumpy," it says in my diary, "amazes [aha!] and delights us with the rapid changes she goes through day by day. Now her smile that used to be a little crooked mouth just lights up her whole face. She looks around for us and when she picks us out she shines a smile."

They change every day, and they learn to smile.

Good role models, I would say.

Here's another thing I picked up in your letter—daughters and staircases. I am flashing ahead a year or two here, but I had to mention this, having been reminded of it. Thea also loved getting carried upstairs, whether I was singing or not. She especially liked it when I invented new ways to carry her. I think our favourite was the upside-down-one-ankle-grip walk. That was a treat you knew would not last more than about a decade.

But by then I was teaching her all the great songs she remembers to this day. She was the only kid in her kindergarten class who knew all the words to "Sunny Side of the Street" and "Up a Lazy River."

But I am getting ahead of myself, aren't I? We are at the moment when our daughter turns three months old. In our case, we had bought the kid a Jolly Jumper and hung it in the kitchen doorway. For the first few times in that contraption, she hung there looking downward and investigating the novelty of the floor. But on her three-month birthday, she did her first tentative little jumps. I just about lost my senses.

I just reread your letter and saw that you found it amazing to watch your baby sleeping on her mother's chest.

Oh, wow!

Your dad-coach—
GB

Dear George,

The yelling and getting yelled at I can understand, but I still can't get over thirty diapers in one day. Were you keeping an exact tally? I feel like it all would have blurred together into a smear of panic and excrement, no? My poop-related worries with Joji tend to come about when we haven't seen any production for a day or two or three—though every book and pamphlet assures us that anything in the range of several a day to once a week is normal (which to my mind renders "normal" a pretty useless category). If I am worried, I seem to have the superpower to summon absolute floods of the stuff simply by voicing my constipatory worries aloud. Take this past Friday: It had been a few days since the little one had dealt any deuces, so to speak, but it had also been a couple of days since her first vaccination, and I was worried that maybe she was having an unpleasant reaction, and said so. There followed a succession of evacuations so massive that—well, let me put it this way: a month or two ago, I read a post on Twitter by a guy named Blaine Capatch that said, "my baby just shit himself so bad i had to wash his hair." At the time, I thought it was funny. Well, now Cara and I have also learned the significance of the final syllable of "shampoo." It didn't help that we were in a hotel, to boot, trying to clean up the mess so that the housekeeping staff wouldn't be exposed to the trace amounts of rotavirus in the little one's post-vaccine stools.

We were a little late getting the first vaccine—about a month. I want to emphasize that this was not a political stand or brought on by any fears of autism or witchcraft. We were just poorly organized. I don't know if you've been following the news about this, but the small armies of anti-social nitwits refusing to give shots to their wee ones have brought about a not-so-minor measles outbreak in the Fraser Valley and on Vancouver Island. Is there any precedent for this, historically? Masses of people voluntarily, and for no good reason, refusing potentially life-saving care? My friend's mother, a public health nurse, once told us that the two groups that simply can't or won't be reached with the pro-vaccination message are the very poor, religious, and uneducated, on the one hand, and the very affluent, secular, perhaps overly educated on the other. The latter group, of course, has no excuse at all—and I'm convinced that this is more of the neoliberal body politics that we saw around competitively eccentric birthing. The thing that really burns me up is the parasitic quality of the whole thing—the way these parents are willing to ride the herd immunity, freeloading on everybody else's antibodies. The recent outbreak seems to have been a bit of a jolting wake-up for some people, which may explain why there seemed to be such a backlog to get the shots. Cara took Joséphine to get her injections on April Fool's day, so who knows what sort of hilarity was going on ...

I didn't accompany the girls; I slept in. All reports are that the baby—who was similarly brave when she got a quick shot while we were still in the maternity ward—cried a tiny bit before going right back to normal. I wasn't there for that, but I was there later on for the borderline fever, which we dealt with by taking off her clothes and other non-pharmaceutical moves, until the following afternoon when we gave her some Baby Tylenol. As I dropped the sticky red substance from a syringe into her mouth, it was neat to watch her whole face take a moment to process the unfamiliar, but seemingly not unpleasant, artificial cherry flavour. Whatever it tasted like, it clearly didn't taste like Mom.

I had three shows in Victoria this past weekend, and our plan had been to go over as a family. We did some second-guessing as to whether it was all that great an idea, given the little one's off-and-on discomfort after the needles, but in the end my separation anxiety won the day. Although we'd both been on the fence about it, and I'd felt like I was about evenly divided between the prospect of a weekend that would be lonely but restful or one that would be family-filled in all the wonderful as well as stress-inducing ways that would entail, when we made the decision to go as a family, my whole body flooded with relief.

It was our first family road trip. I got to briefly share with her one of my favourite experiences in the world, walking out on to the deck of a BC Ferry (the *Spirit of Vancouver Island*, both going and coming back) and breathing in the Pacific and pacific air. She mostly cried through tea at Murchie's, then cried and slept through a trip to Munro's Books, from whose backroom children's section I nevertheless picked up a nice little selection of French and English reading. Later, in the hotel room, I read to her from one of our purchases, a non-narrative book of the French and English words for things. She's never been so engrossed in anything I've read her before. So, it looks like it'll be a career in the federal bureaucracy. Perhaps she can help the young George Bowerings of tomorrow fill out their grant applications.

I can relate entirely to your feelings of total transformation, post-baby. There's a lot of hand-wringing amongst my generation that none of us feels like an adult—we're all just a bunch of Peter Pans. All that angst melted like a spring snow when I became a dad.

And speaking of becoming a parent, two of our very dear friends, Toby and Sarah, welcomed a little baby girl into their arms yesterday. They'd been trying, for years and without success, to get pregnant and had finally arranged to move ahead with an expensive, technologically abetted insemination. A slight scheduling hiccup moved the process off by about a month, and good thing, too—because that's when they got pregnant. Toby joked that they would name the baby in honour of what she saved them: "Ten Grand." But I think you'll prefer the name they finally ended up going with: Thea.

Isn't that a lovely name for a darling little girl?

C.

Dear Chuckster,

I am a little tardy with this segment, because we have been in Texas for the past twelve days. It was a baseball/basketball trip, but as you know, on these trips we also check out art museums and Mexican restaurants. Well, here are my highlights: I saw a Cézanne I had never seen before and got stuck in that room for a while; and we went to a crab shack in Corpus Christi, where I had my first chicken-fried dill pickles. Don't cringe. They are addictive. Jean cringed, then ate half of them.

And I kept joking, "Let's go home. I miss our dog."

But we are not doing a puppy book. We are doing a dad book about baby daughters.

But, jeez, we missed our dog.

I am glad that you mentioned Joséphine's first ferry ride. Can you imagine what the almost-four-month-old tyke makes out of whatever she is seeing, while she's carried around the deck? Gumpy really enjoyed her first BC Ferry ride too, on her way to see her mother's relatives in Courtenay. I think she was impressed mainly by the gulls and their sound. It was around this time, late January 1972, that she was perfecting her pigeon imitation. Immediately before and after all her sleeps she would start cooing, smiling and cooing.

In fact, just around then, when I was facing the dread experience of becoming a first-time house owner, our soft pink offspring with only a skiff of hair hanging at the back of her head was *enjoying life*. It was so nice, amid the lawyer finagling and the expense of shipping our stuff from Montreal and facing the terror of the joint checking account, to look at our daughter's perpetually jolly little face. She had mastered her bouncer, a wonderful relief for a creature who had to spend so much of her life lying on her back or on her tummy.

One thing I was really glad about was that she got on so well with our two loveable Chihuahuas, whom we had had since 1964. They also seemed comfortable enough to share our affection with a third pet. Thea would spend her young girlhood with these little guys, and we had many photos of her brandishing Small in front of her in a modified choke hold that he vainly tried to tap out on.

On that first trip to Vancouver Island, Thea met her first cat. This was Jane, one of the two cats who were living that season with Mike and Carol Matthews at Yellow Point, south of Nanaimo. On the first morning there, while the women slept off a Saturday night of jug wine, Thea and I spent hours together. Her little bald head looked like a roadmap of New Jersey drawn by Jane's scratching as she concentrated in that wonderful way babies have, until on her fourth try, she managed to operate Mike's fishing reel.

"I could do that," I said.

Mike, who had fallen off the porch the night before, had to be reminded of his promise to make Sunday pancakes, so we renegotiated the meaning of the word "morning" and were reminded once more of how much Mike liked to make robust meals no matter the hour. This was the day we found out that a four-month-old can eat part of a pancake with syrup and that a pancake can be eaten by sucking on it rather than chewing.

When I was about four months old, parents tended to have baby books in which they recorded Baby's first smile, Baby's first tooth, Baby's first step, etc. New parents, we know, Chuck, are interested in just about any first that Baby pulls off. I remember the excitement of Baby's first solid poop, for example. So why not a page for Baby's first pancake?

I was also reminded of something by your story about watching

Joji's face as she processed the new flavour of "cherry" medicine. (You see that we are still on the theme of new experiences.) It's a memory I often call up. Gumpy is hanging unexcited in her Jolly Jumper in the kitchen doorway, when I come home with a soft "ice cream" purchased at a "restaurant" in our new neighbourhood of West Broadway. Well, I put that cold white stuff on the little plastic spoon into her mouth and watched as she registered this new page. Her eyes lit up. Her head raised up. She jumped up and became quite jolly.

She was going to spend her early childhood drinking juice instead of pop and all that stuff, but I am really glad in a self-serving way that I slipped her that little shot of smooth sugar when she was a bouncing baby girl. (Hey, while finishing that sentence, I got a long-distance phone call from her. Has Joji made her first phone call yet?)

I was going to add something here, but I've got another long phone call from Seattle, so I think that I will rest here and wait for your next letter, as I always do with baited breath, which is probably caused by the worms I had for lunch.

Your fatherly friend,
GB

April 26, 2014

Dear George,

I am writing to you tonight from Whitehorse, capital of the Yukon Territory in Canada's thawing North—"thawing" both in the general, eschatological-climatological sense of the global warming that has us worrying for all of our babies, but also in the natural, late-April sense that the snow is shrinking into ugly silt piles on the sidewalks and beautiful, shimmering ponds by the side of the highway. Melting, in any case, like a spoonful of contraband ice cream in a baby's mouth. It's funny you should share that story, in fact; just a few days ago, my dad told me a similar one about his mom, my beloved Mamie, who gave me a taste of ice cream when I was around Joji's age. I don't know that today's guilt-mongering parenting experts would approve. I guess Thea and I were just lucky that, given the times, we weren't given drags of a cigarette.

It's Saturday night, and I've been up here since Wednesday after-noon for the Yukon Writers' Festival, doing readings in Whitehorse and smaller (much, much smaller) rural communities of only a few hundred people, where the crowds of less than a dozen folks keep be-ing presented to me optimistically as representing a massive percent-age of the population. Last night's reading in Faro (a village of about 400, down from 3,000, which used to feed workers to the Faro Mine, an operation described to me by one local as once having been "the world's largest lead-zinc mine, now the world's largest environmental disaster") was small on account of a bingo game. Today's reading in Tagish was tiny because there was a car accident, and half the people who were expected to attend had emergency-volunteer duties to do at the site. Even all but a handful of the swans failed to show up—April is, apparently, prime swan-spotting time in Tagish, but we saw only a couple. A local volunteer at the library explained that they might have skipped over Faro this year and gone straight to a place called Swan Haven. Well, yeah—no shit, with a name like that. I'd head there too, if I were a swan.

If my trip to Moncton, in February, was easier than I'd expected it to be, then this was the opposite. It's harder to leave a baby who smiles at you when she sees you in the morning—especially since I wasn't able to wake her up before I left, and had to slip out without a goodbye.

I'll admit that Wednesday night and Thursday morning were a bit of a vacation. My first night in the hotel, I indulged in my own muted form of wild, hedonistic abandon: a few hours of reading, punctuated by unhurried, unself-conscious bouts of onanism. Without any distraction, I read a long short story in *Harper's Magazine*, and throughout, I kept sort of snapping back into my own brain, asking "Where am I?" before realizing that I was in the story. The next morning, as I awoke, my first thought was "Jesus Christ—the last time I was awake was eight hours ago." I felt like I had superpowers.

But what I've found is that you trade a certain amount of your freedoms to have a baby. Then, you fetishize those freedoms when they've been lost. And yet, this week, I've been temporarily re-endowed with my freedoms—I can read and write without having to hold the little one; I can sleep through the night without shuffling over to the edge of the bed during a feeding—and I find that I don't really want them back yet. Not for this long, at any rate. The first day or so was a treat. But I've been dying to get back home and scoop up the little goblin into my arms ever since.

All that said, I think that the break did me good. It came at a great time, anyway. These past weeks have been a sort of mounting shitstorm of work and stress; Cara's been exhausted from full-time parenting, and I've been burnt out from paid work outside the house, and neither of us has really had the resources to help re-energize the other. For her part, the baby is starting to become a bit more like other babies, in the sense that the smiling, cooing, sleeping, and staring that has all been going so smoothly has been joined by a fair bit more crying and fussing. She's still a remarkably easygoing baby—but last Sunday, on Easter, she had a full meltdown at my aunt's place (though it was also Hitler's birthday, April 20, so maybe that's why she was upset). This was the first time since the first couple of nights at home, before the breast milk had fully come in, that we'd seen this kind of sustained, distressed crying—probably forty minutes of it, which I know is absolutely nothing for most kids, but was pretty much unprecedented for us. That feeling of utter uselessness was hard for me to handle, watching my little baby cry and seemingly being able to offer nothing to comfort her. The tears were contagious. Finally, I loaded her up into the car and drove her around the block while Cara got our stuff ready to leave. As I drove, I reached my hand back and gave her my finger to hold in her little hand as she finally stopped bawling and eased into sleep (which she then did for about two hours straight, having expended much bawling energy. She woke up in a golden mood as we were eating fried cassava root and pakoras and drinking chai at one of our favourite restaurants).

I'd like to be able to offer Cara a chance to get away for a night or two to re-charge as well, though it's tough with a milk-fed kid like ours. That said, we have scheduled this coming Wednesday to be a day for Cara to pump and then split, pampering herself with a bit of time. I'll get to spend the whole day with my girl, and I can't wait.

My Yukon loneliness has been technologically abated—whenever I've been within cell service range, which hasn't been all *that* often—by photos and videos sent over the phone, as well as a couple of live video chats (after some technical difficulties when I first got to the hotel). Occasionally, these future-is-now conversations have almost made it harder to be away; seeing her through a cellphone is a poor substitute for smooching her great big cheeks. But Cara did send a clip of Joséphine being swung around in her Tìa Andrea's arms, doing her staccato proto-giggle (it's really almost laughing), and I've watched it about a million times. I watched it in my room at the Mukluk Bed and Breakfast in Carmacks, in a deer-themed room with antlers on the wall and deer-inspired artwork on every conceivable surface. If the buck-emblazoned toilet-seat didn't make me feel far away from home, that video of my grinning little kiddo sure did.

Love,
C

P.S. Writing from the back seat of a taxi, on the way home from the airport. Just got off the phone with Cara, who informs me that Joséphine rolled over onto her stomach this afternoon. If I'd taken the earlier flight—which I'd been offered, but turned down for sleep—I'd have been there. I don't know if there's any lesson to be learned here, but the fact that I'm coming home from the road with a toy rattle that I bought while I was away makes me feel like the absentee father in some unsubtle movie or pop song about seizing moments and being present in one's child's life. I feel like shit, is what I'm saying.

April 30, 20(good lord!)14

Dear Chinook of the North,

First we will deal with this punishing of yourself for not being there for the elf's backflip. You have by now heard lots of remarks about what a swell dad you are, and how you cannot be there every significant moment, you have to be out in the world, performing your duty for Canadian and human culture. I think that Jean said it best when she said she hopes you're not expecting to be there for Joji's first kiss from her boyfriend. (You know, twelve years from now.)

So I was there when Thea did her first little roll-over. Yes, I recall—it was about four in the afternoon on a warm winter's night. She was lying crosswise as usual at the head of her crib, and I had just quit poking her tummy while saying, "Googy googy googy." Over she went onto her tum, and I said to myself, "Boy, I will be eternally grateful for being here to see this." Then I fetched Ange, and we put Gumpy back on her back and I said googy, etc., and sure enough, she did it again. So I got to see the first two. But it was just chance, and I probably missed a lot of firsts, and you will probably see lots of them from now on. If you're home, I mean.

Speaking of Whitehorse, I went there twice, during a neat national event we used to have called The National Book Festival. Writers would be dispatched to various parts of the far-flung country and show up at schools and galleries and other places. I didn't get to go as you did to the smaller Yukon communities, but spent a week at F.H. Collins High School. And boy, did they keep you busy once they had you in the north! Readings all over town, radio stations, newspapers, high school classes, phew.

I was there in April 1982, along with Bill Kinsella, who had got on my plane in Fort St. John (where I'd worked twenty-eight years before). For days we got on very well, despite holding opposite views on almost everything. There was also a poet named Rosalind MacPhee, and I got along with her, though I totally disagreed with everything she said about poetry or poets.

You have to remember that Whitehorse was a lot smaller then, and there were no cellphones, hence no Skype and all that. In fact, in those days I still believed that the telephone was something you used in emergencies. I still hate the sound of the telephone, because I think it means someone has died or is about to. So while I was working my poet's ass off (and taking time to go to the hot springs), my kid, ten years old now, was probably on the ball field, starting her first double play.

Next time I went up there was April 1986. Apparently the kids at F.H. Collins wanted me back, so there I was, fifty years old now and having spent the previous year in Australia, Rome, and West Berlin. Now my companions at the Yukon Young Authors celebration were Charles Lillard and Paulette Jiles, with whom I got along splendidly. Also on the scene was outdoors writer Lyn Hancock, who didn't have time for mingling with poets and novelists. I caught a glimpse of her making sure she had her picture taken with a sled dog. Probably writing a book titled *There's a Raven in My Bra.*

On the other hand, during my visit to the high school I met a beautiful young Native girl who had written a very nice story. She was about Thea's age, fourteen. I wondered what was happening in *her* high school.

The teachers at F.H. Collins were wise and welcoming, and I really liked them, especially Joyce Sward. In 1982, she got a moose roast out of her freezer, and I was a bit nervous. I had had moose once before, and it was stringy and gamey. But the one that Joyce served me was just wonderful, in a northern kind of way. Four years later she had me back for dinner, and this time she brought caribou out of the freezer. It was the tenderest, most loveable slice of meat I had ever tasted. I ate it with a fork alone. If you are one of us people who rate towns and cities by the meals we have there, I hope you were as lucky as I was.

***

Hiatus, while we were in Seattle at a poetry festival, wondering whether we were missing anything our puppy was doing for the first time.

May 5, 2014

Happy *Cinco de Mayo,*

By the way, while we were in Seattle, we put in some time with various little offspring. One was Paul and Meredith Nelson's daughter Ella, who has just turned two. She has had her picture on Facebook every day since she was born and so is quite a ham now. We had a good time playing big-footed monster and escaping heroine. The other kid is one year old and is lucky enough to bear the name Soren, which his parents a little regretfully spell without the ø. This is the son of my ex-student Per-Lars Blomgren, who lives in the family house on Vashon Island, near Seattle, but came to SFU fifteen years ago on a wrestling scholarship, along with his brother Anders. They just kept on showing up in my courses on subjects such as postmodern Canadian poetry, though they would miss the occasional class because they had a Greco-Roman date in some such place as Ellensburg. This kid Soren never stopped smiling his Scandinavian-American smile and splatting his hands on the restaurant's glass tabletop, putting the lie to the cliché of Swedish gloominess.

But you know, I just wanted to get back and see Joji, in case I missed her first, oh, handstand.

But getting back to the subject of being thousands of miles away from your darlings. I hear what you are admitting about enjoying the first few days' holiday. And here is my advice: enjoy them without guilt, and appreciate every minute any time this occurs, because I have news about the future, pal. I am referring specifically to your delighted discovery that "the last time I was awake was eight hours ago!" I am here to tell you that it has been forty years since I had an infant daughter, but the last time I was not awake for eight hours in a row was over a decade ago, when I was lying in the Welland Hospital and attached to a catheter. If you don't catch my meaning, don't fret— one day you will. And our older readers will now.

I am also there to hear your frustration when the kid starts yelling and crying and is too damned tired to fall asleep. I too learned the nearly universal trick of getting the kid into the car and driving around till she falls asleep. I remember doing that in 1972 and being nagged by petroleum guilt. I remember once, in our house on Balaclava Street, imagining throwing her through the window. I wasn't shocked at myself—I knew my love was stronger than any other impulse. I have, though, read the news stories about fathers and stepfathers who shake their babies till they break them. How can human beings do such things, one too often asks.

The next morning, your little human with the big head chortles at you and waves her arms in front of her in that spasmodic way they have, and you want to live forever just like this.

Ole Jawge

May 15, 2014

Dear George,

I feel I've been remiss as a correspondent—it's been a while since I sat down to write one of these letters, and last night, in my dream, you sent me a slightly impatient email telling me it was time to get off the pot and do one. I don't know how this idea got into my sub-conscious; it might've been your subtle injunction yesterday, on my Facebook wall, to "write another chapter in the fiazzakin' book."

But the truth is that I am behind on everything. I had told myself, in the midst of my near burnout toward the end of April, that when I got home from the Yukon I would take at least three days in a row off. Instead, I've barely worked on anything at all since I got back. It's not that I lack for stuff to do: I have two outlines for plays due soon, a book of essays to write, a *Debaters* episode in Kamloops at the end of the month, not to mention our little correspondence here. But rather than getting it together to do some work, I find myself waking up groggily, reluctantly, about twelve-thirty in the afternoon, spending the day in a freewheeling and unaccountable way—walking with the baby, sitting with her out on the stoop of our townhouse as [*Note*: I just returned to this sentence after about a three-hour hiatus; I was about to write about our neighbours joining us to hang out, and that reminded me that I had to be at a membership committee meeting for our housing co-op. I grabbed Joséphine, freshly fed by Mom, who was, for her part, on her way out the door to a friend's birthday party. We went to the committee, which met in one member's living room, where Joji was passed between the arms of the baby-crazy in atten-dance. Afterward we came home, and I gave her a bath—it finally occurred to me to wear a bathing suit when I did so, rather than soaking my underwear with rinse-water—and then we read Richard

Scarry stories and sang Smokey Robinson songs until Mom came back home. Anyhow, all just to say, I've lost my train of thought.] The point is, after the baby goes to sleep, which is around ten or eleven at night now, Cara and I (okay, especially me) stay up stupidly for hours and hours, doing nothing in particular but reading or watching movies or TV. I have yet to figure out how to get work done on a self-directed schedule with a baby in the house. I stay up late, then sleep interruptedly till early afternoon, when I wake up too tired to do anything anyway.

Thank you for talking me down from my guilt about missing the first roll-over. In fact, the guilt had burned off pretty quickly, as I realized that it was silly. Besides, there's some doubt as to how legitimate a roll-over it really was; unlike your experience with Thea, I haven't since seen a successful repeat performance. She rolls and almost gets onto her stomach—in fact, pretty much does, except that she can't seem to get her arm out of the way to make it a clean, flush turnover. For that matter, I have started to believe that to a certain extent, many "firsts" are myths. Take first words, for instance: when she was just a few weeks old, and to our absolutely endless delight, Joséphine let out a series of gurgles that sounded just like she was saying "Oh, good God!" in a Swedish accent. On Mother's Day, I'm fairly certain she voiced something that, ironically, sounded a lot like "Dada," and more than once, including tonight, she has said something that sounds like "Hi." Tonight it was even in response to me saying it to her. Clearly, these don't count as first words, but when she does voice her first words, what'll be the difference? Intent? It all seems very slippery to me.

Or to take another example: This past Saturday, Joji attended her "first protest." It was a rally of a few thousand people and what seemed like a few hundred speakers against the Enbridge pipeline.

The rally was at Sunset Beach, just over from where her mother first clapped eyes on her father, when I was emceeing an anti-war rally when Noam Chomsky spoke to 25,000 people in 2004. But this wasn't really Joji's first political demonstration, since on May Day we had gone down to an anti-pipeline-themed workers' day protest beginning at Victory Square. We arrived, all wholesome, pushing the baby in her stroller, but as we got to the heart of the sparse crowd, we started to have a sinking feeling. For starters, the whole square was ringed with cops; one officer had some sort of camera on a stick and was filming everyone before things even got started. Many of the protesters were wearing masks, and we figured that it was a hotter situation than we could responsibly sign on for. As we left, we had to push past a gaggle of police, and Joji started to cry. Within earshot of the police, in what I thought was a relatively good-natured jab, I soothed her by saying, "Don't worry, sweetie, these guys aren't going to pepper spray you." None of the officers thought that was particularly funny. Turns out I was maybe closer to their intentions than I'd realized. After the protest, footage of the cops roughing up the crowd was uploaded to YouTube, including disturbing images of several of them arresting a young man first writhing on the ground, then, after being violently kneed in the ribs twice by one of the arresting officers, screaming in pain and wailing, "I'm a minor! I'm a minor!"

Anyhow, Joséphine will hopefully be happy that she was at the anti-pipeline protest(s), because this week it was reported that an enormous piece of the West Antarctic Ice Sheet has begun an irreversible disintegration. "This Is What a Holy Shit Moment for Global Warming Looks Like," said the website for *Mother Jones* magazine. I know that every parent, at whatever point in history, wonders what kind of world they've brought their child into, and I know that having a four-month-old during, say, the Cuban Missile Crisis or WWII probably wasn't any less terrifying—maybe it was even scarier. But, Jesus, at least parents throughout history have figured they could promise their kids a relatively chilly polar ice cap. Or sea-level sea levels. Or, for that matter, a Canada that had moved beyond rummaging around on stolen lands looking for stuff they could hock overseas rather than building anything.

On a happier topic, Joji got to meet two of the funniest people in Canada (besides you and me) yesterday, Brent Butt and Nancy Robertson, who are hilarious and married to each other, to boot. Nancy and I are working on a show idea together, and I had to sign some paperwork related to it and get it to her yesterday. I had sent an email suggesting that I would "swing by" with the baby around three-thirty. When I got to the house and rang the bell, no one answered. I knocked, then rang again. Nothing. Joji calmly sat in the crook of my arm while I tried to figure out if I'd made some sort of mistake. I then realized that I'd just said I'd "swing by"—nothing about their house. She must be waiting for me at the café where we usually meet, I thought. Nancy, like you, is not big on cellular telephone technology, so I phoned the café.

"Hi, I think my friend might be waiting for me? Her name is Nancy, she's blonde, might be wearing dark glasses?"

"How old is Nancy?"

"Early forties?"

"Yeah, I think I see her through the window. Hold on, I'll give her the phone."

In a muffled way, I hear the barista ask the woman outside if she is Nancy, to which she answers yes. She hands her the phone.

"Hello?"

"Nancy?"

"Bob!" It's a weird response, but Nancy has a long history in improv comedy, so I roll with it.

"Yeah. I'm so sorry, I'm on your porch!"

"Oh, I'm just at a café." It's becoming harder to get past how much different Nancy sounds on the phone than she does in person.

"Is this Nancy?" I ask.

"Yes."

"Robertson?"

"No."

"Oh, wow," I say, explaining the coincidence. "That's wild! And your name is Nancy?"

"Yes," she says. "And your name is Bob! That's my husband's name!" I didn't have the heart to ruin her version of the story.

After hanging up, I was still no closer to knowing where Nancy was. But I was also getting a small whiff of poop from the back of my little girl. I knew that Brent was on his way to the house, at least, so I decided to change Joji's diaper in the back seat of our car while I waited for him. I got everything taken care of, except that I didn't have a plastic bag in which to dispose of the diaper. Just then, of course, was when Brent pulled up in his car.

Brent got out and came over to meet the baby, whom he'd seen in virtual, digital form on Instagram, but never in person. He was pretty taken with her right off the bat, as most people are. Then his neighbour got out of his truck, carrying a big bottle of blue anti-freeze. Brent said hello and, nodding at the bottle of anti-freeze, asked:

"Whatcha got there? Moonshine?"

"No," replied the neighbour, very literally. "It's anti-freeze."

On the way into the house, I sheepishly asked Brent if he had a plastic bag I could borrow. He casually pointed to a basket in his front yard.

"That's where Oliver's poop goes," he said, referring to his very beautiful pooch. "Why don't you just put it there?"

Not long after we got inside, Nancy arrived home as well (she'd simply forgotten we'd said three-thirty) and cooed over the baby with such gusto she almost got whiplash. Both Nancy and Brent were naturals with the kiddo and fawned over her to the point that Oliver felt he had to come over to me and revenge-flirt. In his defense, he's used to being the cutest thing for blocks, and he even fetches shoes like a cartoon dog, which I saw him do as soon as Brent came through the door.

Joji was an angel for nearly the whole visit, smiling and giggling, even doing her new thing, which is to stretch out her arm to its full length, then fan back her fingers and look at her hand, like she's inspecting a nail job, or she's some adorable fascist dictator. Cara says it looks like she's reaching out to God. Joji got a little bit ornery toward the end of the stay, but I rescued the situation with the classic popping-my-lips-together-with-wide-open-eyes routine that has been a favourite since the beginning. She began to cry in the car until I put Curtis Mayfield's "People Get Ready" on repeat and sang it to her until she fell asleep; certainly one of the most wonderful fatherly duties I can think of.

Love,
Charlie

Dear Student and Companion in Happiness,

We are just back from one of our "working" trips to the south Okanagan, where I was pleased to receive your latest letter. I love this part of my life, when I can look at the little mountain lakes and sagebrush of my childhood in the afternoon and read your excellent adventures in adulthood that evening.

So I want to say that you are not "remiss as a correspondent." Just slow. You are a good correspondent—funny, insightful, loquacious, perceptive, intelligent, and provocative. How do you feel about me as a correspondent, by the way?

I understand how it feels, that terrific demand of all the projects you have taken on, the deadlines, the pressure—and I know what it is like to just goof off with your kid and enjoy doing almost nothing in the spring gloaming. I myself did that for fifteen minutes once, twelve minutes another time, both in 1972.

Yesterday I remembered my very favourite dad-baby activity. I would get the sprat on her back and apply my lips to her bare belly and blow the loudest raspberry I could. She would giggle and wave her arms, and I would splubber another raspberry. That there is something it's worth having a baby to do.

Just this week, on her once-a-week radio show in Edmonton, that former baby played "Slow Poke" by Peewee King and his Golden West Cowboys, and when it was over she said that I often called her that in her girlhood. I have had that song in my head for five days now. "Eight o'clock, nine o'clock, quarter to ten." I surely hope that something like that happens to you thirty years from now, chum. Or this: years ago, I published a short story about a dad who wonders what is happening, and several years later Thea published a short story with all the same characters and events in it but told from the little daughter's point of view.

Still, we are talking about our daughters' accomplishments at an earlier age. I think that yours is the first kid I have heard of who can carry on a conversation at the age of four months. Heck, it wasn't till she was almost a year old that Thea informed me that "ontology precedes epistemology." I was glad to hear that, because I was trying to write an essay about religious thought in recent Canadian poetry at the time.

But while we are on this topic, I hate to have to break the news to you that when Joji said "Dada" on Mother's Day, she was neither addressing nor describing you. She was, rather, naming the art movement that would best portray the life you had brought her into. I know this because on Valentine's Day, 1972, little Gumpy said "Fauvism." During that time I had been dressing myself to look like a painting by Henri Matisse that both Angela and I were fond of.

I can't tell you how happy I am that my little namesake has already lent her voice to a couple of worthwhile political protests. I think it makes for good training. The Gump sat in her little fabric chair on my chest at some of the marches we marched in the early seventies. Now she is a good oppositional citizen, unwilling to put up with any of the designer excrement offered by fast-food CEOs or politicians with Enbridge dollars oiling their pockets.

On her five-month birthday, she got her last needle before the end of her first year, and for the first time her mother managed to bring herself to sort of watch. I have always watched needles, my own and others', but I don't blame anyone who doesn't like to see them. I can't watch any doctor working on my toes.

When I read your dadly missives, I am often impressed by the amount of fun you and Cara are having with this little changeling of yours. I told my diary when our kid was five months old that she was so much fun at times, especially when she was just getting up, all smiles. "When I looked at her last night around two, she momentarily cried hard in her sleep. Angela said she cried all through her first wake up and feeding. The other two times she was all smiles, but later grew cranky before going up to bed. When I'm feeding her, she sits, after her semi-solid food, with no great emotion one way or the other. Then I give her half her bottle and she cries when I remove it for a burp, and she looks over to where it is. Then when it is empty she is full, and she looks at it standing on the table, and she is wistful, but a few moments later she is cheery." (March 15, 1972)

Are you at all like that in your feeding, Chuck?

On March 26, 1972, I managed to arrange for Gladys Hindmarch, who had been the other pregnant woman in our commune, to drive Gumpy and me up to the hospital to see Angela, who was scheduled to have a gall bladder and appendix operation the next day. It would be her first major operation, and of course she was fretting about cancer, as who wouldn't? Right after we got there the nurses, one after another, said that Angela had to get prepped for tomorrow's procedure. We explained that this was her only chance to see her baby for days (or maybe forever, any one of us might be thinking), but they said that wasn't important. It was important to do the shave now because the supervisor wanted to leave at three, forty minutes later. I asked, "How come you can keep Angela waiting two-and-a-half hours at admission, and she can't keep your supervisor ten or five minutes from whatever she was supervising?" Angela was crying as they took her away. Then, as Gladys and I were waiting with that poor little baby for the elevator, a hatchet-faced woman came up to give me shit. She asked why I had made the remark, and I explained that it was a question and why I had asked it. She then informed us that the hospital was not a social club (her idea, one supposes, of the mother-baby relationship) and she had to look after the well-being of her patients. I had to surmise that making them cry as they were forbidden to say hello to their babies was her idea of that.

While Angela recovered in the gruesome Room 888 of the Centennial Pavilion, I bathed and oiled and fed the little one, and found out for the umpteenth time that in caring for a baby nothing is as hard as one had imagined it might be. But the time taken from what one might be doing can be regretted. I figure each kid means one less book written.

No longer pissed off—
GB

June 1, 2014 (but 1:20 a.m., so sort of May 31)

Dear pal,

I just read your letter, and except for the vicious anecdote with the hatchet-faced and hatchet-hearted so-and-so at the end, it made me very happy. I happened to need that very much this week, which hasn't been an easy one—though the difficulties have not been of the little one's doing.

Last Saturday, around this time, maybe a couple of hours later—so Sunday, really—I decided that I should like to have a bowl of yogurt before going to bed. Taking a bowl out of the cupboard, however, I realized that it was already filled with protein: slender white insect eggs and tens of dark little bugs. Cara and I began to unload all of our dishware, dumping it into the sink, crushing the invaders with paper towels, and using our smartphones to Google search just what the nature of our infestation was. My fear—and I think it's a pretty common one on the east side of Vancouver—was that we had bedbugs. I worried about what this meant with regards to our little one's safety. You can tell how worried I was by the text-message exchange that I had with our friend Andrea, who I knew would also be awake at that hour because she'd just had her second little boy, Camilo, and who has an intimate knowledge of bedbugs from her many years as a support worker in the Downtown Eastside. The following are each separate reassurances that she sent me in response to panicked texts and photos of the bugs:

"No, Joji is fine"

"Joji is totally safe"

"Everything is okay"

"Joji is totally safe"

"Stop worrying seriously they r not bed bugs. Joji is totally safe"

"Joji is totally safe. Going to sleep now."

She was right about the bugs. Bedbugs would apparently never have been in the kitchen. We had meal moths.

Then, a few days later, Wednesday night, I was walking home with the little goblin in her stroller. After crossing at an intersection a few blocks from our house, I leaned over—I can't remember whether it was to adjust her hat or to coo, but I've been known to do both on the same trip—when an older man, maybe in his sixties, wearing a checkered jacket, bumped into me from behind. "Oh, I'm sorry," he said, like a pickpocket in a movie. I haven't seen my wallet since. In addition to losing two irreplaceable photos of my late mother (photos that I like to kiss from time to time) as well as my credit card and union card and some receipts I'd been saving for my taxes, I lost Joji's SIN card (not to be confused with original sin, which is what Catholic babies are born with—for this, you have to send out to the government). Now I have to put a flag on my almost-five-month-old daughter's social insurance number lest some identity thief try to take out a mortgage in her name (like anybody from her generation will ever be able to afford to buy a house in this town).

As the week wound down, things were looking up—Cara took a much-deserved break this afternoon while Joséphine and I went for a stroll around the neighbourhood. I listened to a left-wing economics podcast while she snoozed; when she woke up, we sat in a nice little café near our house. I had an iced Americano and a muffin; she had a couple of bottles of mother's milk. We sat on the couch and watched people come and go—everybody seemed to be either pregnant or to have little kids with them. The employees put Marvin Gaye's "What's Going On" onto the record player (they have a real one), and I sang to Joji. Cara texted me that she'd just woken up from a nap and was enjoying the time to herself and that father and daughter should feel free to take some more time if we'd like. There were two bottles of frozen breast milk that she would move into the fridge for us. She might even head over to the walk-in clinic to get the rash that had popped up under her left breast checked out. The baby and I headed to Trout Lake, where we met up with Tia Andrea and her husband, Uncle Derrick, and their two sons, my godsons, and for all intents and purposes Joséphine's cousins. There we hung out until Cara phoned, informing us that we shouldn't use the breast milk that she'd left for us because it turns out she has shingles.

Andrea tossed me a couple of servings of formula for the road as I rushed the baby to meet her mom at the clinic, so that Joséphine could be checked for symptoms. So far she has none, but the doctor put the odds at fifty-fifty that she'll get chickenpox from the expo-sure she had during last night's feedings. Cara's since read and been told some stuff that makes us think our odds are better than that, but we'll go see our family doctor on Monday, and until then Cara's pumping and dumping her own milk, while Joji gets exorbitantly expensive formula made by the good folks at Nestlé or Chevron or DuPont or whoever. Any kissing or holding by Mommy is to be kept to a minimum—the clinic doctor used the phrase "semi-quarantine," if I remember correctly. We both have long weeks ahead of us. Two or three minutes ago, Cara told me that the shingles were starting to hurt a little bit. For my part, I will be assuming many of what have been Cara's usual duties. I'm more than a little afraid—we are a fem-inist household, and we try to be good about these sorts of things, but I've been watching her these past months and there's no doubt about it: she works a lot harder than I do. But I take comfort in your reminder that "in caring for a baby nothing is as hard as one had imagined it might be," which Cara and I agree has been true for us since the start.

I had another worry when the doctor mentioned the possibility of chickenpox, and it's one that I find a bit more disturbing. I worry that the baby might be scarred, and that people may not be as loving and effusively happy to see her as they have been. It was an awful, guilty thought—although I want to be clear that it's not about how I would feel, but rather how I fear people's reactions to her might change. I am aware that we have a very charismatic baby, the kind people really do go pretty crazy for, and I know that her beauty is a big part of that. Thinking of her getting little pocks in her so-far-perfect face reminded me how fickle and inadvertently cruel people can be. I know how much easier life will be if people continue to think that she's beautiful—even if that life, too, will carry its own challenges. You know, it's incredible how *intellectually* aware a man can believe himself to be of how much tougher it is to be a female in our society, only to have it all become terrifyingly visceral when he has a daughter. Suddenly it feels like he didn't know anything before.

[I want to pause here: let's say it's ten or twelve or fifteen years from now and Joséphine has picked up this book and is leafing through it. My sincere wish is that you still get as much joy out of seeing yourself in the mirror as you do these days. Room-illuminating, whole-face smiles. And whether you have chickenpox scars or a goatee, you're beautiful.]

Week from hell or not, you're right, George: we are having so much fun with her. I don't know what else to say besides that. It's goopy and uninteresting to write, but we're just head-over-heels in love with her, and she makes everything better. I constantly find myself overwhelmed by the sheer volume of feeling she produces in me. The Yiddish term is *verklempt*.

As for your question about what kind I correspondent I find you to be, I'm afraid I have only similarly goopy things to say. I worry that if I told you what I think of your letters, coupled with my recent outpouring about baby Joji, that might cause the discerning reader to huck the book across the room for fear of entering a diabetic coma. Maybe we should start writing a parallel series of appropriately world-weary, caustic, and misanthropic letters in order to keep our edge?

Edgily yours,
C.

June 9, 2014, the day before my father's 107th birthday

Dear Charles, as in Olson, as in Parker, as in Reznikoff, as in Demers:

When I was a kid I really enjoyed reading the Bible, getting those *stories*, hearing those *poems*, looking at those *pictures*. Some of the stuff scared me, like the way the Hebrew children went into the promised land and killed everyone and took their grapevines. I consoled myself by understanding that I was a kid in a democratic world, where the bad guys in Europe were being stopped by us heroic Americans and maybe a few others.

One of the things in the Bible that most impressed me was leprosy. I understood it to be a biblical disease, but I had asked, and my dad said that it was still around, although it was not about to afflict anyone in the modern sanitized world we lived in with bathtubs and so on. (I think he may have been encouraging me to get more personal with the bathtub.) There were islands in Hawaii and near Victoria, where there were still old lepers acting out the ends of their lives, lives that would remain mysteries because you were not allowed to visit these islands. Somehow, whether from the Bible or the dictionary or at Sunday school, who knows, I learned that the first thing that happens when you get leprosy is that some part of you, usually a hand or foot, turns white. That means that you are beginning to suffer from leprosy.

So I kept checking my extremities, and I noticed that if I held the palm of my hand up and spread my fingers as hard as I could, the middle part of my palm started to look a little white. I walked around in solitude, as I often did when I was a kid, in this case attendant to my secret martyrdom. I think this was the dark side of various secret thoughts I had in those years before and after grade one classes. I thought that I might eventually find out that I could fly. I was the first human being to be immortal. I could not rule out the possibility that I was going to be the second coming of Jesus Christ.

Years later I settled for being able to write books that got published and occasionally read.

Well, leprosy wasn't the only Biblical thing I thought might operate in my life. So if you think that you are Vancouver's leading hypochondriac, I am going to ask you: did you ever think you were a young leper? I am often accused of being psychosomatic when it comes to illnesses, but of course this is not true. And perhaps I join you in thinking of ordering a personal tombstone that reads: "See? I told you. Bubonic plague." As I wrote on the first page of one of my books, I could not eat raspberries until I was in my thirties because when I was around four I swallowed a raspberry and in that instant thought that there might have been an insect in the concave part. So it is with amusement that I follow your adventures in trying to stay alive, and it is with sympathy that I read about your projected hypochondria for Joji. I remember lots of occasions such as this:

"Holy Moses!" (This was before we all started exclaiming OMG!) "Look at the colour of this, oh, you know, some little piece of furniture ..."

"Stool."

"Yeah, stool." (Because "stool" sounds more medical and therefore more serious than "poop.") "It's a weird colour. What does it say about purple stool in the baby doctor book?"

"She had Gerber's beets for the first time last night."

Similar scenes were acted out after Thea started teething on wax crayons.

So now you see that we have got this correspondence back to the subject of baby daughters. But I remember that it was I who suggested that you write about getting pickpocketed. I figured that it would get you started on another chapter, and it worked. I deeply admire the way you managed to get my little namesake and the pickpocket into the same sentence. I haven't been pickpocketed, but I was mugged in Seville by a young asshole on a motor scooter, and I had my man purse stolen in the pink Safeway on Broadway. It feels sort of like having been assaulted, doesn't it? When Angela and I first lived in Montreal, Expo was on, and the buses were crowded, and I said to her that she should be more attentive to her handbag. "Pfft," was what she said. Sure enough. I almost felt good about having been right, but then I had to figure out where to borrow some money for groceries in a city in which we had not formed all that many friendships yet.

Most of all, I wish that you hadn't lost the pictures of your mother. That sort of thing is not going to happen in the future. Your little inheritrix has already been in more pictures that the previous six generations of her families. Of course I don't have as many pictures of my baby girl, though I remember taking film cassettes to the drug store every couple of weeks. But there are surprises: just this week there was a snap on the web that I had no memory of. It shows a very cool dad (me) and daughter (maybe nine-year-old Gump) flâneuring along some maybe European street. Yesterday I sat for a couple hours in a restaurant with my old classmate John Boone, looking at pictures from our high school days. Keep snapping, young chum.

Well, then along come (comes?) shingles, and maybe along comes chickenpox. The only experience I have with shingles is watching Angela get them when a certain good friend who was going through some very annoying years came to stay with us for a while. I don't know where we got the idea that shingles are psychosomatic responses to stuff, but I also don't remember whether Angela ever had the chickenpox when she was a kid. I did. In my day, you expected to get everything; every kid did. Mumps, chickenpox, red measles, German measles, ringworm, scarlet fever, etc. That and operations for adenoids and tonsils and appendix. Plus the other things you got only if you had bad luck, like rheumatic fever and so on. Ah, and broken bones and scars.

But what caught my eye in your narrative was the brave lamentation that "any kissing or holding by Mommy is to be kept to a minimum." Assuming that that applied also to Joji, I was put in mind of the days leading up to weeks after Angela had that gall bladder removed, this while Thea was a babe (not) in arms. I don't remember how heavy she was at five months, but her mother was not allowed to hold her, so I used to stand behind Angela and reach around and hold the baby in front of her so that she could put her arms around the tot and pretend that she was holding her up, and then she could do all the goofy noises that parents make when they are interacting with a baby. Let's just say that for the next month and more yours truly did all the heavy lifting.

Oh, but getting back to chickenpox. I don't think you get scarred from chickenpox. It's smallpox that you get scarred by. Well, you also get dead from it. It's up there with leprosy.

Oh, and why spend all that angst on what your perfect little girl is going to look like fifteen years from now because of chickenpox? I mean, how much worrying do you do about whether she'll have your nose?

Yours in the hope that pickpockets really, really need the money—
GB

Oh, and here's a tip for the future. If you think that viruses and the like are worrisome, in a time that will seem shorter than it does now, your kid will be driving a car on some highway in another province, at night.

Dear George, as in George I, as in George II, as in George III, as in Bowering,

Let me start by saying that I still haven't fully given up the possibility that you may be the second coming of Jesus Christ. So—no spoilers!

As a kid, I had an illustrated children's Bible that I too quite liked. (I appreciate that in Christianity, children get their own Bibles, Crusades, etc.) A while later, when I was seventeen and hadn't thought about them for years and years, the pictures in that book came back to me when I was in Jerusalem—it was my first time ever overseas, or in a place under military occupation, for that matter. Although I was, by that time, like most teens, intellectually committed to atheistic Trotskyism, the religious sights were still pretty jaw-slackening. That said, I did slip and fall on the smooth, polished floor of the enclosure in the Church of the Holy Sepulchre, which I did not take as a good sign. Perhaps a punishment for future blasphemies, like ascribing potential Christliness to one George Bowering, humanity's first immortal.

A few people have already pointed out the biblical quality of the past few weeks of my life, since my last letter—I've drawn at least one comparison to Job, and a Facebook friend raised the fact that my days seemed to be ominously filled with pox and flood.

See, I'm writing you now, George, not too far from your place. Cara, Joséphine, and I are in exile, renting an apartment at UBC while a crew of workers tears out the warped floors and potentially mouldy walls of our recently flooded townhouse. The asbestos tiles came out yesterday, to my great surprise—for starters, I'd had no idea we had asbestos *anything* in our house. But after an insomniac night,

Cara had decided to let me sleep in, and when she finally woke me up around noon, the first word that I registered was "asbestos." I grilled the poor guy removing the stuff for a long, painful time about why it would be okay to do it with a little baby in the house. He—and everybody else in my life who knows anything about the stuff—finally managed to convince me that everything was all right. It's something called non-friable asbestos, and it pretty much never gets airborne unless you saw through it with power tools. Still, as a fellow hypochondriac, I'm sure you can relate. While I want Joséphine to be in touch with her Quebecois heritage, I draw the line at asbestosis.

Asbestos Day was precisely one week after Father's Day—my very first, of course, and spent, at least in part, carefully painting my baby's chickenpox with calamine lotion, using a Q-Tip.

As it turned out, we didn't really end up quarantining Mom from daughter all that much while she had shingles—many sources explained to us that it is very rare for a child to contract chickenpox from a parent who has shingles, and our GP wasn't even fully convinced that they were shingles in the first place; if they were, they were the mildest case he'd ever seen. He let Cara go off her anti-viral prescription, and so Mom and baby were able to start breastfeeding a lot sooner than we'd thought. Happiness came back into the house. We basically wrote off chickenpox as a possibility.

So confident were we that we even convinced ourselves that the two little reddish blemishes that popped up on Joji's right cheek just before we left for a party at our friends' place weren't anything to worry about. We called ahead—there would be other babies at the party, including the hosts', still a few months too young for his chickenpox vaccine—but decided that this was just another case of projected hypochondria. I felt even sillier when we got to the party and the host-baby's face was covered in heat pimples and blemishes far more dramatic than Joji's. We entered, we mingled, we waved the little one in front of grown-ups and kids alike. Then, being a good dad, I went to change my daughter's diaper and, lifting her shirt, saw a pocked little belly with a small constellation of little pink dots. We shot out of the party like a toy hurled from a stroller. Even the next afternoon, when Cara took Joji to the walk-in clinic, the doctor couldn't say for sure whether they were chickenpox—she had none of the accompanying symptoms, and besides, he hadn't personally seen chickenpox in about a decade.

It wasn't until the next morning, my first Father's Day, that the subtleties dropped away as the little one erupted in spots. It's no leprosy, chickenpox, but I tell you, for such a mild and relatively innocuous virus, it sure does look for all the world like your baby is oozing and melting under the effects of some medieval curse. That said, I needn't ever have worried about how people would perceive her, scars or no scars: people cooed over the pocked-up photo we posted to Facebook as much or more than any smooth-skinned images we'd previously posted. My little kiddo is unflappable; almost always smiling.

There was no fever besides cabin fever as the three Ng-Demerses found ourselves sealed off from the outside world. It wasn't a perfect seal, of course—we visited adult family members who'd already had the virus—but, as it turns out, it was better than whatever was joining the pipes in the wall we share with the neighbours behind us. Midweek, in addition to the varicella bubbling up from underneath my daughter's skin, I found bubbles and puddles of water spurting up between the tiny cracks in the laminate flooring in the living room. Over the next few days, crews came to pack up all of our downstairs belongings, march them out of the house, and replace them with giant air purifiers and dehumidifiers. I've worried about Joji inhaling mould, then asbestos, and then, just a few hours before we left the house for UBC, I got a call letting me know that my dad was admitted to the emergency room after having thrown up and with a mild fever. They kept him there overnight, hooked to an IV full of antibiotics. On both sides of the country, neither grandfather nor father nor daughter were sleeping in their own beds.

I was worried, of course, about my dad. Still am, although they sent him home this afternoon. We'll get the test results of his CT scan and biopsy—results we were already waiting for before the latest episode—in the next few weeks. I am easily shaken by any news from my dad, and yesterday was the first bit of tough stuff to deal with after a string of very optimistic weeks.

My father and my brother both tend toward positive thinking—although my brother admitted to me that this was about simply not allowing himself to go somewhere that he can't handle going. I am the only catastrophist in the immediate family, though my maternal side is relatively full of them. Still, I find myself either dreading what's happening with Dad, or else it leaves my mind completely. It's funny—because of losing Mom so young, I had always sort of assumed that the universe, or the guy in the Bible, would never even consider taking my father from me prematurely. It's almost impossible for me to separate out thoughts of her death, and my loss, from thoughts of my dad's illness or my daughter's life.

A few weeks ago, I explained to my psychologist how I'd broken down in tears in the middle of the night, watching Joséphine cry because she was given bottles of formula rather than her mother's shingles-stricken breast, and my doctor pointed out to me the fairly obvious metaphor of the situation. Motherlessness. Two generations behind me, on my maternal side, are parents who didn't make it out of their thirties: my mom was thirty-nine when she died; her dad, my grandfather, was thirty-three. I turn thirty-four in about a week.

So I'm working on it with my psychologist. I don't want every moment that I spend with my little girl to be spliced in two, as it so often tends to be: the joy of the moment itself and a simultaneous, nostalgic mourning for it, even as it's happening.

Moments like this, one of my favourite from the past few weeks: Cara was at the stove cooking, and I was behind her, holding Joji. I could see that the little one wanted to touch her mom, so I brought her closer. Cara turned round, and Joji reached out and touched her with her hand. Then she turned to look at me, reaching out to touch her dad. Then she turned to look back at Cara. She seemed to be processing us as two separate but somehow related units.

I said to her, "We're your two."

And then I started to cry.

Love,

C.

Dear Father Figure,

No, wait! Let's not mention figures. But hold! Isn't it mothers who worry about their figures after having a baby? I do remember the case of Sergio, though. Remember the baby Ximena in México? Her father Sergio was a yoga instructor who did breathing exercises with Ximena's mother Meg right up until the happy event. Anyway, you have heard about fathers who have sympathetic morning sickness and sympathetic labour pains? Some time after Ximena's birth, Sergio had sympathetic stretch marks. I told him that I thought that was taking identification too far, but I *was* impressed.

As I write this, you are purportedly at your little family retreat on Galiano Island, while your home dries out and so on. But I am suspicious. Last time you were on a retreat over there, we were there too, and you were up at four in the morning, writing your East Van Panto. I was up at ten, looking for an ocean-side breakfast. Like the US troops in 1816, I know how to retreat.

You can't imagine how happy it makes me feel to find out that you fell down in an important building on your virgin trip overseas. I have fallen down in many important places. I fell on my face on the stone walkway, among many well-shoed feet, right where Dante met Beatrice, according to Henry Holiday's famous painting. According to the painting, it was a lot less crowded at the end of the thirteenth century. As soon as I got to Havana, I went for a drink in the lobby of the hotel Hemingway liked, and fell on a coffee table, thence onto the stone floor. At Beijing's Forbidden City, I fell on my face and camera, right beside a sign that indicated that it was forbidden to fall down. I also fell on my face and camera and the stones in Willemstad, and had to forego the Curaçao baseball game I was aiming for. I have often fallen face down on domestic sidewalks, of course, but who celebrates the customary? So, welcome to yet another club, Pops!

Just to say, I will always think of you as a stand-up guy.

I was glad you brought little Joséphine over to meet our giant pup Mickey. This was the latter's first close-up meeting with a baby, and as you saw, she was very much impressed. Later she told me that she wished that she spoke baby language, because she wanted to show Joséphine how to use her back foot to scratch at her pock marks. I was also impressed by your coolth: Jean was holding the baby, as mothers seem to like to do, and you were not leaning forward with grabby hand while Mickey snoofed the cute little creature. I was nervous, thinking about the way Mickey likes to hold her rubber ducky by the head. Unless you are a great actor, I was more of a special kind of hypochondriac than you were.

Anyway, good on ya for getting through chickenpox. As my parents used to say regarding all four of their kids, "That's *one!*"

Rereading your letter, I start to wonder whether you are having an accelerating version of my life with a kid and home. I spent, with my female partner and offspring, a lot of years in a cavernous house on a corner in Kerrisdale. Quite often the aforementioned female partner decided that the gargantuan house had to be changed. So bathrooms appeared in new places, paint replaced wallpaper and then was replaced by new wallpaper. Walls had holes cut into them, and fluid insulation such as was normally found in Saskatoon pumped into them. Then a few years later the walls came down as the insulation with the comforting name of urea formaldehyde was removed. The expanded suite installed in the basement filled knee-high with liquid shit after the next-door neighbours did some excavation for a swimming pool. I will just mention this small sample, not the elevator and the added balconies and sun salons, and the upstairs floods, etc.

So I know about moving out for a while. I know about loud machines blowing or sucking air for weeks. I know about trying to get the infant used to this year's version of a back porch. I am hoping and predicting that while you may catch up to me in face-dives, you will be able to get by with normal occurrences of munching insects and undulating walking surfaces.

I didn't write poems or stories or personal essays about all these domestic adventures. I should have been the comedian my schoolmates expected me to be. "So, a man's home is supposed to be his castle, am I right? How come no one ever told me about the moat I have to cross after every spring run-off?"

Or I could have been a sailor.

Now it is July 7, and according to someone with your name on the antisocial media, you are *en famille* in a hotel where early-morning deconstruction is happening. I presume that Cara told you this when you woke up five hours later. I sympathize. A couple decades ago I was in Vancouver General Hospital for possible death, and shared a ward next to the five-in-the-morning horror machines that were building a new pavilion. I was longing to get home and listen to my Neu! and Kraftwerk albums.

But then there are those moments such as the one that ended your most recent letter, so long ago. A very touching moment, and now you know why such moments are called touching. That is a new person's voluntary sense, and one can tell that this new person is saying yes, I can make my action affect the world. Ironically, it is the one sense that is totally reciprocal. The new person feeling (transitive) is also feeling (subjective). The toucher feels touch. I remember figuring this out when I was six months old. In fact, I wrote a paper on it, which my superstitious mother destroyed.

You will remember (because I keep mentioning it) that when

Gumpy was six months old, Angela had her gall bladder operation at Vancouver General Hospital and was frustrated because she could not carry the kid, which is apparently something mothers like to do. So while Angela was in the hospital, I had to stay in the house, and even after she was home, I had to stay within a few blocks, because Gumpy woke up so often. On the first day home, Angela tried a little baby lift, and learned why she had been advised not to try it.

Looking now into my April 1972 diary, I see that things seem to have changed about feeding babies. Thea was a Gerber baby, or whatever brand of canned baby food we used. I imagine that like a lot of others things we used, such as urea-formaldehyde insulation, canned baby food was really, really wrong. We had a forward-facing baby seat in the car, for heaven's sake! My diary also tells me that I enjoyed shopping for cans of baby food and trying Thea on this and that. One day I got her some rice pudding. Apparently, she liked just about everything we gave her (a trait that would continue into her childhood), but she liked everything else better than meat, except for ham. Of course, when she got old enough to switch to the red cans, known as "junior food," we found that they didn't do ham any more. She liked fruit the best, especially peaches. I thought that this might have been because her father was born and raised in the Okanagan Valley.

Meanwhile, my lifetime habit of staying up late at night was over. If a late movie on TV threatened to run past one, I tended not to watch it. Well, unless it had Charles Bronson in it.

Cheerio, lad. I know that you don't have any worries about pockmarks on your daughter's face or belly. You don't have any psychic scars, do you?

Georges

July 24 (well, after midnight—so, 25), 2014

Dear Coach,

Thank you for your patience in awaiting the correspondence that was your due—I wanted to write from a time and place other than the Job-like space in which I've been stuck for the past month-and-a-half, schlepping our possessions from place to place, trying to keep one step ahead of structural water damage that seemed to be following us across the city, living without any dependable physical space in which to write or relax, fraying at all my edges. I am pleased to inform you that tonight I will sleep, as I have for about a week now, in my own great big bed, with only a few items still in boxes and a few paintings yet to be re-hung in an otherwise-returned-to-normal world, in a relatively dry household, with a relatively dry sense of humour about the whole thing. We have brand-new floors, across which our now almost-crawling girl can pull herself without fear of drowning or knowledge of the breaststroke.

The month started off, as you point out, on Galiano Island—starting, as July often does, with July 1, my birthday. My first one as a dad was a great pleasure. The weather was beautiful and Cara brought Joséphine down the stairs in a pretty dress and wearing her beautiful hat (I think the one you guys brought her back from Mexico) and gripping the envelope containing my card, on which she'd drawn a few squiggles, and containing the promise of my gift (baseball tickets, to see our—yours and mine, I mean—beloved Vancouver Canadians). We hit an important milestone: when I was a kid, if a grown-up lay lengthwise on the couch with their knees up, the triangle that they created with their thighs, calves, and the back of the couch was called "the cuddle spot" and considered perfect for seating us little ones. On my birthday, I had the honour of providing Joji with a cuddle spot, in which she managed to sit for even longer than it took to take a photo. We had my birthday dinner seaside at the Galiano Inn with our—yours and mine, I mean, plus Jean's and Cara's—friends, Lee and Jim. Some dinnertime screeching by the baby gave her and me the chance to go outside, for her to get spun around aloft in the air for a few turns, and for me to consider how lucky I am to be *a* father in general and *her* father in particular. Joji loves being held up to fly, and the only way she loves it even more than normal is if she has an audience for it. When I lift her up above my head, she straightens out her body and lifts her head, smiling—then casts a quick look around to see if anyone else is taking it all in. If there is, we get a second smile.

The week on Galiano was idyllic in roughly this way—Cara holding Joji as she kicked her feet in the tidal pools on the rock beach and Dad swam in the cold water off the shore, etc.—until near the end of the week, as a few of our friends—as in just mine and Cara's, this time—arrived to spend the weekend with us. Just as our pals pulled into the cabin's driveway, with Cara upstairs getting changed and me downstairs coming out of the bathroom, I heard one of the most spine-crawling, nauseating sounds I've ever heard (and keep re-hearing): the sound of our six-month-old daughter rolling off the bed onto which she'd been placed while Cara changed her shirt and hitting her head on the pinewood floor. Say, have you ever been to the Galiano Medical Clinic? Fine facilities. Luckily, the baby was okay, but we were given a list of warning signs to keep an eye out for and, well—you can imagine how well that went over with your fellow hypochondriac. The creeping anxiety of the next few days set the tone for our return home to the scuzzy hotel that you read about on Facebook, then over to the basement suite of our friends' place (the same friends who came to visit just as the baby was crashing onto the floor), then finally back to our place. Last night, I was sitting on my cherished leather recliner couch watching TV until relatively late at night when I heard that same sick-making sound of a body crashing off the bed coming from upstairs, only this time much more dramatically. I ran upstairs in a full panic, knowing that Cara had been nursing the baby before they'd both passed out on the bed. As I arrived panting in the doorway I discovered the baby lying perfectly still and calmly in the middle of the mattress; her mother, though, had half-awakened from a chasing dream and pursued the game off the side of the bed and onto the floor. (You were so enthusiastic about my falling story, I figured I should provide you with some more.)

You mention Thea and her easygoing eating habits, and it reminded me of a story you once told me about teasing her for always ordering the grilled cheese sandwich Pirate Pak at White Spot (which is what I always ordered as a kid, too). "You can have a grilled cheese sandwich at home!" is how you explained your mockery to me—but did it ever occur to you that this meant your own grilled cheese-making skills were wanting? Anyway, I stand with Thea.

Joji has had her first tastes of solid food this month; once with our permission and premeditation, the other without. We had planned, after she turned six months old (which she did on July 3), to feed her something like banana or avocado, which is what we went with, a few days ago at my aunt's house. We mushed some up into a bland, single-ingredient guacamole and spoon-fed her the good green stuff with my now-eighteen-year-old cousin Aedan's old baby spoon. She took a bit of time to figure out the process but seemed to like the stuff, and we continued to feed her until she lost interest. This was almost exactly how we'd planned her first taste of solid food to be. Only this wasn't her first taste of solid food.

We didn't want to give her anything on Galiano, on the off chance that she'd inflate like a blowfish from some unforeseen allergy, with us separated from the nearest emergency room by a body of salt water. But Galiano is, in fact, where she got her first taste of grub, in the arms of our old family friend and Grey Cup-winning BC Lions alumnus John Pankratz. I've known John since I was a little kid, but I'd never had any reason to discover, before this trip, that he is baby-crazy. He and Joséphine were mutually smitten from the word go. He held her and entertained her for a huge chunk of the week we spent on the island, and when he held up a shortbread cookie that he was eating for her to see, I didn't think much of it. Then he let her smell it, and I thought, *Wouldn't it be funny if he let her try to eat it?* Then he lifted it to her mouth. It was a much bigger hit than the avocado, I can promise you. The first time it was taken away from her, she cried. Eventually, she had to be distracted as it was removed from the scene (I think John ate it). As I think I mentioned earlier, my grandmother gave me a taste of ice cream when I was around that age, and God knows I've never had any issues with overindulgence.

The baby has entered the second half of her first year, and the pace of change seems to have sped up considerably. As I mentioned, the kid is, if not crawling exactly, able to move herself without anybody's help from one part of the floor to another. Sitting is executed with much more confidence, as is grabbing, slapping, and stroking. The ambivalence that once dominated her attitude toward toys is gone. The largely helpless, mostly inert little infant of just a few months ago has been replaced by a sturdy kid with a whole range of skills involving arms, legs, and head movement. She kind of waves, too—though it sometimes reads like she's trying to reach out and touch whomever she's greeting.

That's been the wonderful part of the last few weeks. Here was the most heartbreaking: A six-month-old Palestinian baby in the Gaza

Strip, Musa Abd al-Rahman Abu Jrad, was killed in the recent Israeli bombardment of Gaza. I wasn't prepared for how reading that would make me feel, George. This kid, who would've gotten started living and breathing within just weeks of my little girl's birth, who should have been her contemporary on the other side of the world, whose parents should have been thrilling to roughly the same milestones as Cara and me for the next few decades, is already gone. I don't usually cry when I read the news, but I bawled when I read that. Went upstairs and woke Cara and the baby, just so that I could hold her. I'm still reeling from it. A stranger on Twitter told me that having a child changes the way you watch the news, that I should hold my daughter tight. It's true, and I did, but it's small consolation for Musa's parents.

Besides Musa, the other baby I saw in the news this week was the royal baby, Prince George, "greeting his subjects," in the words of the news anchor. Babies being killed by the army in one place, a baby ruling over his subjects someplace else. Quite the little civilization humanity's carved out, huh?

Love,
Papa

Dear Job,

(And remember, a Job worth doing is a Job worth doing well. I take it that you are well done, as opposed to, say, "Oh rare Ben Jonson!" That famous quotation, misspelled there, is above Jonson's tomb in Westminster Abbey, where he is the only person buried in a vertical position. So you might say that this playwright, famed for his comedies, was a stand-up comic. Forgive me.)

So it is with great levity that I acknowledge the hassle your life has been the last little while. But I did see the Facebook picture of our Joji making her way across your new floor. You are right—it is not quite crawling, but a kind of crooked sliding and pulling. I believe that this locomotion falls within the boundaries of what they call creeping. In fact, we were told that it was a baby-book truism that the kid had to learn to creep before learning to crawl, and learn to crawl before learning to walk. If the critter skips one of those stages, it was said, bad things would happen in the course of her development— adult bedwetting, perhaps, or excessive tattooing, or taking up the accordion. Watching Fox TV. I was really happy that Thea crawled a week before walking in our living room.

Before that, we had her in one of those weird little card tables with a square hole in the middle and castors on the ends of the legs. The kid sat in a chair in the hole, and propelled the table around with her feet. Thea usually did this stuff on the back deck, usually sideways. She loved it, and we thought we were so smart buying the latest in 1972 baby gadgets. Then someone gave us a recent issue of *Consumer Reports*. Apparently this vehicle had been responsible for more baby deaths and injuries than King Herod.

But the last you heard of my youngish dadhood was around her six-month birthday. I managed over time to get almost used to being up before God was awake in the morning, and feeling sleepy early at night. My late-night movie and talk-show watching habit was pretty well gone after a couple of weeks.

I got to know her better than I had ever known a member of my family, especially when it came to things that this young mind was learning to like. On Sunday, April 17, 1972, I made a note of some of the things Gumpy liked. Here I will slip into the present tense:

> She likes to stare at light bulbs, any strength; when you walk with her from room to room she gawks around, looking up at what seem to be her personal deities. She likes to grab or hit any dangling noisemakers. In her room she has Tibetan bells, in the kitchen dangling shells, and in the front room the hanging bamboo. At first she tentatively reached out for them, but now she grabs them with lightning speed or smashes them with a haymaker right. (This was before we found out that she was left-handed.) She likes to scratch as many surfaces as possible with her fingernails, including walls and two Chihuahua dogs. She likes to take her bath on a towel in a few inches of warm water in the upstairs bathtub. She likes to eat peaches, but doesn't care all that much about meat. She likes to start in on a loud screeching session after meals, happy screeches that get louder and louder. She likes to knock down the tower you build with her rubber blocks. She likes her grandmother Lillian Luoma. She likes men with beards. She likes to stare at her shadow, especially if it moves. She likes to give airplane kisses, to anyone, mouth open, including her reflection in the bathroom mirror.

I guess any family with a baby knows about airplane kisses, though they may have different names for them.

So your six-month-old likes to fly like a plane (and this before she had her first flight in one) in your hands, and mine liked to kiss like a plane. Boy, daughters and airplanes, eh? Later on, I have to warn you, it gets to be daughters and horses.

Well, we are all here to say that flying is better than falling. I can't remember how often we heard a thud in the bedroom, but it wasn't all that often in the first year. I have to admit, though, that I fell out of bed all through my childhood. Sometimes I woke up and was surprised. Sometimes I said to heck with it and slept on the floor. My parents got a woven rug and placed it beside my bed. I never broke anything falling out of bed, and I don't think I ever had a concussion. Later in life, I got a concussion playing soccer on the Okanagan Valley rocks when I was in grade four, and another on a New Year's Day in Vancouver while walking off the ball diamond after the third out that was not noticed by our jejune first baseman.

I don't fall out of bed nowadays, though I expect to. I save my falling for places built on stone or concrete. The only fall I am really interested in is the fall in gasoline prices.

Who can explain kids and Pirate Paks? This week, a former student of mine brought her nine-year-old all the way from Liechtenstein to a White Spot restaurant, where he had his first Pirate Pak, and guess what he had in it? Fish! We all have our Pirate Pak stories, I guess. Having a very fast operator as a dad, my daughter didn't know for the first year that you got a chocolate-like coin as part of the deal.

Speaking of food, I have to say congratulations for going with home-mushed vegetables and fruit instead of Gerber's. I don't know whether one should really be afraid of that pap conglomerate, even while noting how easy it was to go along with their neat little jars, but one should be aware that one of the other businesses Gerber is in is life insurance.

And without a decent segue here, let me pause to remark on your knowing John Pankratz. As you know, I am not a big fan of football, especially of Canadian football, which is played during baseball season, but as an English professor I had some contact with a few CFL players and future CFL players. One was a fullback (or whatever they are called now, inside exterior fallback receivers, maybe) whose name I don't remember now, who scraped through his freshman English course and later played for the BC Lions, I think. Another was Sean Millington, who played a dozen years in the CFL and later had the vocabulary to do TV work.

But the most interesting was Rick House. I recognized his name from the early days when I watched a little football, even occasionally in a stadium. House was a receiver who won two Grey Cups with the Winnipeg Blue Bombers and one with the Edmonton Eskimos. I met him when he came to SFU to take my course on contemporary Canadian literature about the time his gridiron career was in its last phase. He had a good attendance record and seemed to be working pretty hard on Margaret Laurence's fiction or whatever it was, and I liked him, his presence in the classroom. But for his term essay he was more congenial than expert, and I gave him a grade that could best be described as "feh." When he finished his final exam and handed it in, I took it with a sore heart. But when I read it I was gratefully astounded—it was an A exam. Later I asked him how come he did way better on the exam. It was usually the other way round, I said. He told me that his wife couldn't help him on his exam.

Rim shot here.

As to all those Gaza children being blasted apart or left to live a traumatized life, you are exactly right about being a father seeing that news. Then, like me, you will grow older and feel despair that this hideous thing is still going on after all these years. And you never will lose your awareness of any daughter's fragility.

Tearfully—
GB

Dear George,

I sat down in order to write to you almost a week ago, from Halifax, Nova Scotia—something that has become a bit of a habit, it seems. The biblical story of my life as a father has moved from the tribulations of Job into more Exodus-style wandering, as our little family has made its way across Canada by airplane and automobile, with stops in Toronto, Montreal, and now the jewel of the Maritimes (don't tell Moncton I said that).

I meant to write you from my dad's living room in Halifax, but I didn't. Then I didn't for several more days after that, even once I'd got home. But I didn't—because George, I'm just so tired. I am so very tired.

I can't forget that early moment when Cara turned to me and said, "Isn't this way easier than you thought it was going to be?" My answer to her question was affirmative. It was easier than I'd thought it was going to be—and not by a little bit. It was *much* easier.

I think when you think something like that, it starts to frame how you process everything that comes after it. In some ways we were right: Joji is a much easier baby than most—laid-back and, thankfully, unbothered by health troubles or any evident trauma at having been evicted from Cara's uterine Eden into the cold world. But what I don't think we realized was that the challenges of parenting can be acute and they can be chronic. If you're lucky enough to avoid any work that feels too overwhelming to do in the moment, it may still be overwhelming in the sheer never-endingness of it. It's easy to stand on one foot for ten seconds. You might even turn to your standing-on-one-foot partner thirty seconds into it and say, "Isn't this easier than you thought it was going to be?" See how you feel after an hour.

The (mostly wonderful) multi-city visit back East also made clear just how much help we're missing out on by having no grandparents in our time zone, or even in adjacent ones. Did you know your grandparents well, George? Did Thea know hers? I was raised thousands of kilometres from my paternal grandmother, who was in Québec speaking French and voting for political parties with blue in their logos, but from ages three to eleven, I lived in the very same house as my maternal one. That multi-generational set-up seems to me eminently more sensible than the solo-flying model that appears to be preferred these days (by people who, maybe not coincidentally, often feel more comfortable just having the one kid).

To see Joséphine in the arms of her grandparents, and even a great-grandparent, was a treat beyond any words I have at hand. These weren't airplane kisses, but post-airplane kisses. Incidentally, Joji was a champion air traveller, even despite a new set of slobbery physiological challenges. As the aircraft lifted its nose out of Vancouver on its way to Toronto, I gave the baby my pinky finger to suckle in order to keep her jaw moving against plugged ears. *Say*, I thought to myself as I felt the inside of her mouth, *it didn't used to be so sharp in here.* All of which is to say that our girl has a new nickname that she likes smiling up to when called One-Toothie Ruthie.

It was after midnight Toronto time when Joji landed in her Poh-Poh's arms, and Cara's mom was filled with a deeply touching love and enthusiasm that carried us through the potential stresses of her not knowing exactly where it was that she'd parked. Slightly more disconcerting was the fact that the car seat that she'd lined up, and had had installed by the family friend who'd lent it to her, seemed to lift up pretty effortlessly off the back seat. Since it was too late to sort out any alternative plan, I drove home in paranoiac style, with hands at ten and two, before finding out the next day that, in fact, and as I'd suspected, the seat hadn't been installed properly. It took us several more days—days filled with bus rides and subway rides—to get a new seat sorted out. As she is everywhere that she goes, Joji was a big hit among her fellow passengers on Toronto's public transit system—like the man on the subway who clapped his hands and said "Here!" to the baby, outstretching his arms as soon as we sat down next to him, and who had to be let down easy.

Cara's mom was adorable to watch with the kiddo. Like someone aware that she doesn't have as much face time during which to establish her grandmotherly bona fides, she went into charming the baby purposively, with her elbows swinging, and the gambit paid off. Joji was fully smitten with her within a day or two and gurgled with delight at the Cantonese rhymes that Poh-Poh would rattle off for her.

The whole family set off, after just over a week, to Montreal, driving Poh-Poh's car—and at more than one point, I was chauffeuring three different generations of sleeping Tong/Ng women. It was also around this time that Joséphine developed a three-day-long propensity for flipping the bird. When finally we got to Ste. Thérèse, sitting in my grandmother's living room as she spoke *des mots douces* to the little babe, I watched as Joséphine responded to her great-grandmother by gently extending her the middle finger. *Tiens-toé, tabarnac!*

My grandmother's name is Alberte, and her grandmother's name was Joséphine. Initially, my dad was supposed to drive out and meet us in Montreal to make it a four-generation affair, but his continuing health troubles made it impossible this time around. Then, on our last day in Montreal, barely twelve hours before our flight to Halifax to see him, Alberte woke me up early (like, probably ten), to tell me that I had to speak to my dad. That it was important. That I should sit down.

Dad's graft-versus-host troubles, arising from the stem-cell, bone-marrow transplant that he had received from my aunt just after Joséphine's one-month birthday, had presented themselves in three spots: his liver, his mouth, and on his skin. His skin had essentially been burned from the inside, left cartoonishly red and dappled with white spots. His mouth is incredibly dry, filled with mostly useless and unreceptive taste buds. His liver—well, I don't know. But it's his liver, and it's pretty important that it works.

And unfortunately, it wasn't working the way that it was supposed to. Nor was it responding as it was supposed to, to the treatment he'd been receiving. So now they wanted Dad to come back into the hospital, and maybe he wasn't going to be able to see the baby at all. Did we still want to come, or should we change our flights and go back to Vancouver? I hung up the phone and sat in sad, scared, tired contemplation in my grandmother's chair. It seemed to me that it didn't make any sense for us to turn around and go home, but if he ended up quarantined, I didn't want to torture him with the knowledge that the baby was just a few feet away but might as well still be on the West Coast.

We tentatively decided that we would come anyway, which turned out to be the right decision since later in the day we found out that Joji would be allowed up on his hospital floor, and that he might even get day passes to come out and see us. We got to Halifax after midnight, and the next morning I woke up and headed downstairs with the hopes of going to see Dad at the hospital. Instead, there he was, on a day pass. I threw my arms around him, then rushed upstairs to get his granddaughter so that he could begin his week-long swoon.

I was initially worried that Joséphine would be afraid of my dad's odd colouring and extreme skinniness, but I needn't have. The only real worry arose in relation to a relatively minor health irritation, when the tingling in his left foot caused him to fall on the rocks next to the lighthouse at Peggy's Cove. He was holding the baby when he went down but managed to keep her safe from harm by sacrificing his knees, which became scraped and bloodied. Dad was so embarrassed about falling that I swear he complained more about that moment in the week that we were there than I have heard him complain about his lymphoma over the past few years.

I've just realized that it's 10:37 p.m. Halifax time and that I haven't phoned my dad yet, and besides, the café where I'm writing closes in twenty-three minutes. So I'll wrap things up pretty quickly. I will say that I couldn't ask for anything more than having seen my father and my daughter have the week together that they had. I asked Dad at one point what it was like being a grandfather, as opposed to a father. After a second's thought, he described it with the phrase "compounded exaltations."

We even did a visit to his hospital room, where Dad and I made the mistake of trying to feed ol' One-Toothie Ruthie a serving of strained sweet potatoes; the kiddo instead discovered the catapult principle, sending the stuff up to the ceiling where it splattered next to an inspirational quotation written above the window facing out to the Atlantic ocean: "We cannot direct the winds, but we can adjust our sails."

Love,
Charlie

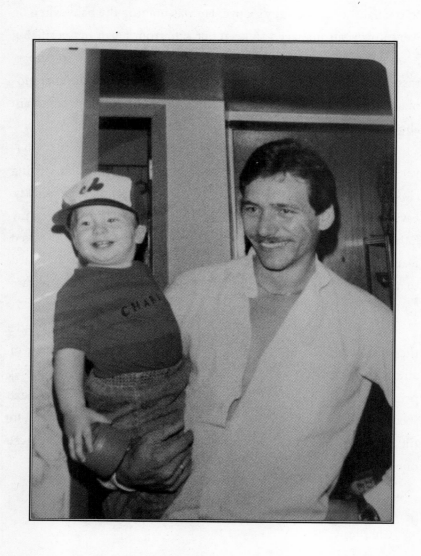

Back from Oliver

August 27 (my favourite number), 2014

Dear Charles,

Have you checked to see whether Joji has slender ankles, or is it a good thing for a baby to have slender ankles? What I mean is that Persephone, the lovely and famous daughter of Demeter, was beautiful and had slender ankles, according to the Homeric hymn addressed to her mom.

I was thinking of this earlier in the week because I was up in Oliver for a kind of family gathering, and Thea was there from Edmonton, and I noticed for the umpteenth time that she does not have slender ankles if you compare them to her father's or her uncle Roger's, whose ankles are famously skinny. But I did see her in her eyeglasses for the first time. I kept asking her to put them on because she looks so forty-two-year-old beautiful in them.

What I am leading up to is that maybe you should look into the idea of having a poet write a hymn to your daughter. I know that our daughters will be incredibly thankful to have this book about them, but what female person does not dream about somebody writing poems for them? King Lear might have stayed out of trouble if he had hired a hymnist, I'll bet. Well, I will leave that up to you.

Of course, no one, much less your fatherly correspondent, is going to be as predictable as to say I told you so about the business of being very tired. We just sympathize. I am so glad that Angela had her debilitating operation during the semester in which I did not have classes to teach, so that I just had magazine deadlines and publisher deadlines and CBC deadlines and cooking and laundry and shopping and gardening and cleaning and so on after all the diapers and feeding and burping and napping and so on. By the last week of April, Gumpy was sleeping in till seven-thirty or eight. According to my diary, "I don't notice myself being any more rested than during the six o'clock mornings," and, "I've been going to bed as early as midnight, and that is indeed strange." (But you must know about people like Corporal Donovan. I knew him in the air force in Manitoba. One year, his wife had twins. Next year, she had a baby. The year after that, she had twins. Five gifts from Zeus or whoever, and the eldest two years old. I hope they all had slender ankles.) That April I had little baby flower seedlings in cut-open milk cartons on windowsills all over the house. The sort of thing idle, contemplative people like to do.

I am glad that you introduced the subject of grandchildren. And am interested in the idea that you introduced it in terms of "how much help we're missing out on." There were a lot of Bowerings in the south Okanagan when I was a kid, and there are still quite a few. I got to see my dad's parents a lot. They lived in nearby Summerland, and when I was a young boy before working age, I'd stay with them for a week or so in the summers. My grandfather, who got around on crutches, was the post office man and had been a Baptist preacher before that. My grandmother taught me to knit, often called me by her youngest son's name, and being a devout Christian, was shocked that I was reading a book called *The Gashouse Gang*, not realizing that it was about St. Louis Cardinals baseball.

As to my mother's family, we saw them much less often, except for the few that were in Penticton. Mom's mother died when she was an infant, and we seldom saw her father, who lived with another wife and a lot of the Brinsons in the Kootenays.

As for Thea? One of her grandmothers, my mom, is ninety-eight years old, and they saw each other this week in Oliver. They enjoy one another on the yearly occasions when they meet. My father died when Thea was two, I think, and though he had been here in Vancouver when the Gump came home from the hospital, Thea doesn't have any memory of meeting him. I don't think that she ever met her grandfather Luoma, a dark Finn with an unstable presence in the world, but she knew her Nana, who lived in Vancouver for part of her life. In fact she was once in a group of four female humans who represented four generations, the earliest of whom had been a young woman in Scotland. But Nana was starting to cope with multiple sclerosis, though she did not know its name at the time, and she never did the famous grandmotherly business of babysitting. Thea was very fond of her, and remains very fond of her one living grandparent, driving two days from Edmonton to see her each summer.

Meanwhile I can't get my mind around the fact that one of my grandparents died ninety-seven years ago! Her ninety-eight-year-old daughter sometimes tells me that she is looking forward to seeing her again.

Oh, we rime a little, don't you and I, we fathers of daughters, and I suppose that is inevitable. My daughter did not hurl baby food onto my dad's hospital room ceiling, but she did visit him there. He had had a heart attack on the Comox golf course and was trying to recover in the hospital there. Little Gumpy was a biped by then and could say some words. "Hello, Gampy," is what she said on that occasion, and he answered to that new cognomen. A few months later he came back from a golfing trip to the California desert and died in the hospital where Thea was born. Before Dad went into VGH, my parents stayed with us in our new house with almost no furniture in Kerrisdale, then moved for a while to the apartment of Jamie Reid's wonderful mom Eunice near the hospital. Toddler Thea didn't know a lot about what was happening. Neither did I, and I was in my thirties.

Oh, and teeth? Let us go back in time a year. I can tell you that the Gump got her third tooth on her mother's thirty-second birth-day, May 5. The little seven-month-old wasn't feeling too good. Her mother was developing a new feeling about breastfeeding.

Charlie, get rested in little bits as you can. Here is a passage from my diary for May 22, 1972:

> Some irony here. I'm slaving over Blake's *Songs of Inno-cence*, and I can hear my baby cooing downstairs and I want to be with her, but I don't let myself because I am conscious of Time pressing me. I decided to cover *Songs of Innocence* and *Songs of Experience* and *The Marriage of Heaven & Hell* yesterday and today, poor benighted hope, there is so much to expend on every word, and I'm sup-posed to have Williams ready for tomorrow's class, too. And I must have a bath. And it was a lovely sunny day but I had to miss most of it. Up here in my study overlooking the noise of the Greek restaurant-bar.
>
> Thea today learned to grind her four teeth, a noise whose charm will not long outlast its first five occurrences.

The next day I went to my seminar to learn that my students had not got around to reading the Blake poems. For this I had lost a day in my toothy daughter's life.

Your biggest fan—
Grumpy

September 27 (your favourite number?), 2014

Dear Grumpy,

It's perfect that your most recent (but not *so* recent) letter ended on a note of a young father trying to get work done in his creative life and to be a good dad while having his limited Time and his limited energies sopped up by sometimes-Sisyphean teaching duties, because that's pretty much exactly why you haven't heard from me in a month. It's not that there haven't been things to write about: Joji's steadfast refusal to let us feed her solid foods (though she will still always strain her tongue to lick any facecloth or anti-eczema cream with which you wipe her cheeks); her pulling herself up to standing, first in her crib (requiring the lowering down of her mattress), then against stairs and, last night, the coffee table (which she was gnawing, in seeming contravention of her strict stand against solid foods); her second tooth; the filling-in of her somehow-golden dark brown hair; and the rattling off of syllables, "Mamamamamamama" and "Dada-dadadadadadada" that have been hopefully interpreted as direct and purposeful addresses. It's just that there hasn't been any Time or energy with which to write about it.

Here's an emblematic instance: Last Saturday, I was hosting a variety show just off Commercial Drive—comedy, staged reading, music. Cara and Joséphine joined me at the show, although the two of them got locked out of the building after making what was supposed to be a brief exit for some air, while the baby was letting out some of her now-trademark staccato screeches. When she came back in for the second half, Cara was tired and in need of a break, and so I took Joji up on stage with me for my second monologue. This was her second time on stage, the first having been the night of her two-month birthday. She had slept through most of that set, getting a few good laughs by waking up at just the right spots, in an early display of comic timing. The audience loved her that time, but I'd say they probably liked her even better this time around, fully awake, though sometimes scared of them. "This is Joséphine," I explained, "she's named after Stalin." That's a joke I've been making for a while, but this time I got to add the true events of the preceding night, when we had introduced her to an old Trotskyist friend at the annual general meeting of the People's Co-Op Bookstore, who had narrowed his eyes when we told him her name, and asked suspiciously where we'd gotten it (it's a good thing he didn't notice her toy ice-pick).

I then explained to the audience that we'd opted not to get a babysitter for the evening, as my aunt and uncle had babysat for us the previous week, giving me the opportunity to humiliate myself as a solipsistic young father. As I was listing off all the babysitting essentials—here's where the formula is, here's where her diapers are—it struck me that my aunt and uncle, who'd had two boys, might not know all the intricacies of changing a baby girl. "Now, you've only had sons," I said, "so, do you know about wiping poop *away* from the vagina?"

"Yes," replied my aunt, citing experience with her *own* vagina.

The second half of the variety show went off nicely, but in the middle of the last act—a full-dress mariachi band called "Los Dorados," who between numbers would tell the mostly *gringo* audience about mariachi history; did you know, for instance, that the trumpet was a relatively late addition to mariachi, opposed by some traditionalists at the time? It's as hard to imagine mariachi before trumpet as it is to think of my family before Joji—received an email on my phone from one of my teaching assistants explaining that that week's required readings were not in the course pack. Another of the readings had been printed twice, instead. So now, after the show, I had to drive across town to the university, arriving after midnight, to scan copies of the readings and email them to the entire class.

To be honest, George, I'm glad to be writing you only now, because I haven't been in a good place this past month. Actually, I would say that I've been miserable. Not in relation to the baby—she's the only thing in my life to which I've been able to reliably turn for any kind of happiness or strength to keep going. But I've been desperately regretting my decision to take this teaching job, which was supposed to be part-time but is swallowing up everything. The weight of several writing deadlines has been constricting my chest—all stuff that I was supposed to get big chunks of finished during the summer of Job, but instead did virtually none of between the flood-dodging and the travel and the raising of a child. Sleep only came in small pieces and had started to fill with recurring, deadline-influenced dreams of people waiting for me while I failed to do whatever it was that they were waiting for me to get done. Then I got a cold and couldn't shake it, I'm sure because I wasn't resting. I have been as tired as it seems possible to be, at all times, for as long as I can remember.

A few things have brightened the past couple of weeks. Remember my wallet, which was pickpocketed from me as I leaned over my baby girl's stroller at the beginning of the summer? As it turns out, no such thing happened: I'd lost it in the park, where it had been found and then turned in to the front desk of our local community centre, in whose safe it had been sitting for two months as calls were placed repeatedly to a landline whose voicemail we never check. More significantly, things have recently taken a very good turn with my dad, whose medical team is thrilled with his progress.

Another is that my darling Cara and I have stepped back from the brink. For a few dark weeks at the end of this summer, it seemed impossible that we would stay together. We were like two people pushing cars with empty tanks side-by-side up a steep hill and somehow still managing head-on collisions. Someone would irritate the other, who anyway was waiting to be irritated, and then we'd hurl exhausted viciousness back and forth at each other till we stopped. The time between truces contracted significantly. It seemed that at least once a day, or every couple days, one of us would say that we didn't think we ought to stay together—and we would say this totally passionlessly, once things had calmed down. That was the terrifying part.

A fight on our way out the door to the doctor's office for an all-family check-up was our rock bottom. "You're *horrible*," I'd said to her on the landing, straight from my viscera. In the car, as I drove— she in the back seat next to the baby—I tried to take it back, clearing the way for cool-headed discussion by saying, "Look, we're two peo- ple who love each other—"

"I don't think I love you anymore, Charlie."

It was "anymore, Charlie," that lacerated me. The phrase made the sentence so much more realistic, and intimate. "I don't love you!" could just be a childish outburst, and patently, provably inaccurate. But "I don't love you *anymore, Charlie*"? That's resigned, reflective. And in the moment, superlatively believable. And relatable.

I think we were both rattled by that particular exchange, and af- ter emotionally and lovingly walking the whole thing back, we silent- ly, tacitly agreed never to let it get that bad again. We've been more generous with each other since, and very loving. For all my com- plaining about life in general, I'm a very lucky man. My psychologist tells me that statistically speaking, the most difficult times for most couples, those that put the most strain on a relationship, are when they have very, very young children or teenagers. So we've got that to look forward to.

Oh, and by the way, Mr Coy, don't tell me I should find some poet somewhere to write a tribute to my kid—you're still, by my count, the biggest poet to come out of Oliver, and you've met my darling girl. I can't really tell what kind of ankles she's got, though—well, except that they're perfect. Like her hands and her eyes and her hair, and pretty much everything else I can think of.

Love,
Father-of-the-year, Husband-of-the-afternoon

October 10 (an important date for me in 1952), 2014

Dear Child, as in the child is father to the man, or as Mrs Wordsworth had it, the daughter knows what you are all about:

As our plane was entering the sky above Houston last spring, I was surrounded by people who were coughing loudly, and I correctly predicted that I would have a cold in a couple of days, and the cold lasted three weeks. As our plane was rising above Bavaria a couple of days ago, I was surrounded by coughing people, and now I am on the first day of my fall cold. I feel especially distraught about this because it means that I will write a crummy letter to follow your magnificent last letter. So I apologize, but I don't quit.

Funny vowels going on around here. You and I referred to me as "Grumpy," to which I offer no defence, and my baby daughter's nickname was "Gumpy," and the first time she ever said something to her Gramps, she called him "Gampy." I have to say that during much of this month's vacation in Italy, I could hardly walk, and my travelling companions called me "Gimpy."

I'll call you Child.

See what you cook up.

Or otherwise prepare for that gnawing kid. She is going to eat solid food, starting with semi-solid. Maybe she is already doing so, since your most recent missive. I would like to suggest *purée de pied de table*. Not all that nutritious, but toothsome. With Gumpy we didn't have trouble because we were living in an age when it was still all right to gorge your kid on bottled pap, alternating with bananas, steamed turnips, father's scalp, and other soft mouthables.

That gnawing does not mean that the kid is lacking plywood in her diet, but that she has to exercise those new teeth. Teething is the name of an exciting time in parenthood. The mother, for example, enjoys dentation during breastfeeding, and the father endures finger pain as the price for his new pride.

About five years later, there is the excitement you feel when those now loose teeth finally fall out, to be replaced by an uneven array of new enamel. That's when you collect the replaced bicuspids in a plastic pillbox along with the first hair clippings held together with an elastic band. (We will probably not be writing this exchange when that happens, so I won't be able to tell you about Angela's lack of enthusiasm when I told little Thea about the Snot Fairy.)

I envy you your experience of carrying the kid on stage, which would make more sense if she were Candice Bergen (though she'd probably be kind of heavy—and I wonder whether this jest is too rarified for the general reader). During my twenty-year class reunion, many of my former classmates were surprised that I had not become a comedian. I did not say anything about the fact that such a remark suggested that they thought that I would become an unknown comedian instead of an unknown writer. What I mean is that my kid didn't get in on my act until she was about eleven, when I would ask her to handle some of the entries in a poetry contest I was judging.

Anyway, I was seriously moved by your letter, by your telling the story of the strife with Cara. I know that your shrink is right in saying that parents of newborns (and especially firstborns) can have this experience. You know, of course, that a significant percentage of the world loves you two and cheers for you, and you probably know at bottom (hey, I can use whatever word I want) that Hemingway was right—you are stronger where you were once broken, like bones. And this: I've been there and then some.

I have just been looking through my diary from the period when Thea was about eight months old. Ha ha! I can report that a week short of her eight-month birthday, she sprouted her fifth tooth. There is no report of gnawing, but there is the recorded fact that she had a new custom of wearing her square pink-rimmed sunglasses whenever she was eating in her highchair. Also that she used her (now illegal) walker to chase poor newly walking Lars (Gladys Hindmarch's son) all over the commune. I remember feeling an apprehension that she would never learn to play hard-to-get.

Not that she was just a rowdy. On June 5, 1972 I bought Angela, who thought that she'd better learn to drive now that she had a kid, a racy white 1969 Sunbeam Alpine GT. Gumpy had an awful time that day, being startled over and over and made to cry and cry. First, for example, the billowing curtains at the open window beside her change table. Then the air horns and telephones at the car dealer's. Then the billowing curtains near her bed. Isn't it awful when your little girl is frightened? I never before felt such empathy—is that the right word?

Oh, over the years it would be more than frightenings.

I note the importance you attach to the first explorations your kid makes into the world of words. It will be even more exciting, I can tell you, when she lets you know that she gets the sentence, that imitation of relationships. You could jump on this and get her speaking a Chinese language as well as English, because they both go noun subject-verb-noun object. French? She'll pick it up the way all our kids do, eh?

At nine months little Thea could use simple word-sounds to designate Angela and me, as well as our dogs, and the birds we'd show her (this was back when there were birds in Vancouver yards). She also learned "bye-bye." You might say that she was at the stage where our sixteen-month-old Bernese Mountain Dog was at a year.

On July 19 after feeding Gumpy, I said, as I always did, "all gone!" While I was putting her dish into the sink I heard her say, "da dawn."

Then she said, "Da Dawn!" Then "ᴅᴀ ᴅᴀᴡɴ!" Then "DA DAWN!!"
Etc.

More or less the way I was learning to write poetry.

Looking for an early reply,
I remain your admirer,
GB

Dear friend Charles who begat little Georgie or some such name:

This morning, while sitting on my poetry-reading seat, I put down Pierre Reverdy and began to have a reverie about my baby pictures. Until I was about six years old, my parents used their small bellows camera to make a lot of pictures of me, their first-born. During my first year there were a lot of pics, and quite a few the second year, and maybe a few fewer the next year. My sister appeared with me quite often when I was six and she was five. A decade later, after my two kid brothers were born, their pictures were pretty well left up to me and my Baby Brownie.

It had been no easy thing, making pictures of little chubby me. While home photography was a popular hobby, it was pretty expensive for a schoolteacher during the Depression. The camera could not have been cheap, and there was film to buy and prints to order. My father's salary topped out at ninety dollars a month, and there was half a year during which the school board in the middle Okanagan just plain ran out of money, and my dad had no salary at all.

So those pictures have always been precious to me. Maybe if there had been digital cameras capable of storing hundreds of shots in colour, the pictures wouldn't have seemed so special.

I still had to rely on film thirty-five years later, though I was now using a 35-mm single lens reflex to take a lot of black-and-white snaps of little Thea. And sure enough, I took as many pictures of her in the first two years as I would in the next ten.

I guess one is glad to have the pictures one does have. And nowadays babies are all over the internet, as popular on social media (as it is called for some reason) as kittens and plates of food.

After a while I got up from my poetry seat and started the rest of my morning routine—wash and dry face, wet down hair, drop in eye drops, suck on inhalator, comb hair, take two kinds of hypertension pills, take a Tylenol 1, maybe brush teeth, swish non-alcoholic mouthwash, step on scales. Shower and clothing will happen after a day's work (at the moment of writing this letter, it is 3:40 p.m.).

While I was doing this, I continued my line of thinking. Writing, I thought, was something I took up doing professionally after photography (given some of my photographic assignments in the Forest Service, Air Force, etc., I might have come upon the news that writing is less dangerous, too). Specifically, writing about my kid was something I did a prodigious amount of at her birth, and which I did a bit less of as she grew and her consciousness began to move in with mine. I often wish that I had kept a journal devoted to her young life. Instead, I made observations about her in my diary, along with my softball games and lists of people I had talked with at poetry readings. I am really glad when I look back at that diary and see a reference to Thea's doing something that I had forgotten. When I do that, I wish I had elaborated and continued such observations the next day and the next. Any reader would have seen the value of my preoccupation.

On July 30, 1972, when the little tyke was nine-and-a-half months old, I was fitfully marking papers all day, and the day just went away. I stopped to make some supper, and just before supper I was in the kitchen, listening to the radio with Gumpy. I was about to turn off the radio when she gave me a stern look, this little bald baby, so I left it on. On came my interview with broadcaster Jurgen Hesse about the Kosmic League, our guerrilla softball disorganization that was into its second season with expansion teams in East Vancouver and Burnaby. So there we are again.

A week and a half later, my diary notes that Flex Morgan had defeated us (the Granville Grange Zephyrs) 27–10, that I was in the middle of marking papers, and that, "Gumpy was wearing Kali's old string dress this morning, and she looked really neat." Kali's father, the Toronto poet Victor Coleman, had given her the dress. I wish I had a picture of it, but it helps that I have this little sentence to remind me of a connection I wouldn't have remembered.

And then there is this: it won't be long until my brain not only quits remembering but quits operating. But then Thea will have pictures to look through and words to tell her things she will not remember doing when she was in the first year of her life.

I wish my father had kept a diary about us kids. You think?

With fatherly care,
GB

Dearest George,

I don't know what to tell you—I feel like I should be writing to you with news of Joséphine's second marriage, or *her* kid's teeth, I've let so much time go between letters. I'm ashamed to be responding to not one, but two in a row from you. I sincerely hope that I'm a better father than I am a correspondent. That said, there's something to be gleaned from the tectonic, widening spaces between the dates on my notes to you—I read an essay a little while ago that mentioned the Nilometer, the measuring technique used by the priestly caste in ancient Egypt to record water levels in the Nile in order to better predict what a given year's crops might look like. Similarly, I think that if an Egyptian priest measured the growing distance between my correspondences, he might get a pretty good idea of how a father's first year gets swallowed up.

Does that make any sense, what I just said? It makes sense to me, but I can also see how it makes sense only with the kind of stoned, dream-logic of the hyper-exhausted. I got your Candice Bergen reference, at least I think I did—it was about her father having been a ventriloquist, right? I had a replica Mortimer Snerd dummy when I was a kid, which I chose on Main Street, USA, in Disneyland, at the age of ten; then I learned from books how to speak without moving my lips. I'm now trying to figure out how to live without moving my body.

September and October disappeared like a Kleenex in a campfire. I know that I've mentioned this before, that in my pre-fatherhood cluelessness and naiveté, I signed on to far more work than I could handle this autumn. I am teaching two courses at UBC and a non-fiction workshop at Simon Fraser University, writing one play that goes up in December, another that goes up in March, a book of essays, and still doing a few (though not as many as I ought to be doing to stay in form) stand-up shows, in and out of town. I flew to Nanaimo after my last letter to you, to tape an episode of *The Debaters*. The week after that, I did two left-wing fundraiser shows in Regina. Last weekend, I drove an hour to do a show in Squamish, which happily I was able to drive home from on the same night. The poster for the gig billed me as a "Shrill Leftist & Family Man." Our baby girl has now figured out that I am the parent who leaves, and this knowledge manifests itself in ways that absolutely slay me, in good ways and bad. When I'm home or out with her, she often clings to me in an intensely daddy's-girl way, sometimes doing her best to avoid letting other people hold her, including her mom (her ever-present mother gets taken a bit for granted, unless it's been a few hours since she's seen her—then, it's as if a switch goes off, and "Where's Mom?" becomes the pressing question at hand). Anyhow, that's the beautiful way that my girl's consciousness about my sometimes having to leave is manifested. The heartbreaking one, the one that wrecks me, is the crying and yelling as I leave, sometimes accompanied by reaching out and grabbing the collar of my sweater, pleading with me to stay. A few weeks ago, I got to class at UBC (I'm pretty sure that I'd been crying in the car on the way over), and I began by telling my students that they had to be brilliant that day, that they had to be worthwhile and engaging, because I was only there over the screaming objections of every biological impulse in me to have stayed at home cradling my baby girl after she had begged me, in her way, to stay. It kills me. Kills me. Every time. Usually I'll surrender for a few seconds, taking her from Cara to hold her close, give her kisses, before handing her back as the wailing starts right back up at the same pitch.

So why did I agree to this punishing workload, knowing that

there'd be a largely helpless little person hanging around, whose twenty-four-hour-a-day well-being was roughly fifty percent my responsibility? Part of it, I guess, is that—cliché of clichés—you never really know what it's going to be like until it happens, the vacuum of time that your days become. But I also think part of it comes from trying to emulate my own father's example—my dad who, when I was a kid, had a wife in the hospital, two children, and a full-time job, and who was going to school full-time on top of that. Somewhere I got the idea that a person could simply will themselves past exhaustion, defy gravity. It's not really how it works. Things got really bad for a while; I was crying at the drop of a hat, always tired. It's been better for the last week or two, though it's not totally clear to me why. In a moment of sanity, I stopped myself from quitting my job at UBC. That decision should pay off big time next year when our family is, you know, eating groceries and living in a place.

I did have one little bit of out-of-town work that seemed to be a happy turning point, because I got to take Cara and Joji along with me. We went up to Whistler for the writers' festival there, and got put up overnight in a swank hotel, the Fairmont Chateau Whistler, and Joséphine got cooed at and held by some of the bigwigs of Canadian Literature (besides you and me, naturally). The Whistler trip was also a big turn in Cara's mood—I'm happy to tell you that everything continues to improve on that score, and that the feeling of love and of being on the same side continues to grow, for which I am deeply thankful. More sex would be nice, of course—but we'll get there. From what I hear from other new parents, we are far from exceptional in that regard.

There was a weeklong visit from Dad, and my brother had a benign tumour removed from his pituitary gland, though not in that order. It's been such a delicate goddamned year for health in this family of mine, and none of it helps my propensity toward emotionalism. But Joji loves her Papi and her Uncle. She also loves climbing up the stairs from our living room to the front landing (this has become an obsession, and we had to put a gate on the stairs, the erection of which happened to ironically coincide with the week of the twenty-fifth anniversary of the fall of the Berlin Wall; Joséphine looked at us as though we were the Stasi). She loves to be read to, giggling through her favourite books. Her two most beloved titles are a call-and-response book in English, about the body, called *All About Me*, and a wonderful French-language book that I picked up while we were visiting my grandmother in Ste. Thérèse last summer about two pebbles who fall in love. She has lost all her skepticism about solid food—now she tastes and chews on everything, from kamut toast to wooden toys. She has the most interesting way of tasting things, holding them in the fingers of her right hand and curling her wrist in almost completely, then poking the foodstuff onto the middle of her tongue. It never gets old to watch. Oh, and our first Halloween! The kiddo was supposed to go as Kermit the Frog—a tribute to one of her favourite songs, "The Rainbow Connection"—but at the last minute, my aunt's sewing machine broke. Happily, Joséphine had inherited a sea otter costume from our friend Wayde Compton's daughter, Senna, which not only fit perfectly but kept my little one warm against the pre-November chill.

Today rehearsals started for the play I wrote that goes up in December. It's a kid's play, another East Van Panto, like the one we did last year, only this time, instead of "Jack & the Beanstalk," we're doing "Cinderella." It's a trip to be coming up on another Panto, because Cara was pregnant in the lead-up to last year's, and the run of that show coincided with what had been almost guaranteed to be Joji's birth—in fact, I'd written in the program that my daughter would be born sometime during the run (we remember how that went). Well, this time she's here. We're hoping to take her to opening night. I had wanted to take her to rehearsal today, but was told very gently by my friend the director that that probably wasn't a good idea.

Rehearsal was fun, except that toward the end, I found myself on my cellphone embroiled in a fight on Facebook (you're absolutely right, George—I don't know why they call it "social media"). The fight revolved around the reaction to a shirt worn by a scientist. This week, a bunch of European spacemen landed a rocket on a comet. It was big news, and one of the male scientists went on TV to talk about this big news while wearing a short-sleeved, collared shirt covered in sexed-up drawings of comic-book-style women. A number of people rightly pointed out, as my friend Tabatha Southey did, that hundreds of thousands of little kids were watching this breakthrough moment in space exploration, and that perhaps this fella's shirt didn't send the most welcoming signals to potential young scientists of the female persuasion. To his credit, the fellow has since apologized, but that hasn't stopped other men from making a big show of how they don't find anything to be offended by in the whole scenario. This is a really strange cultural development: people want to be acknowledged as somehow brave or bold for managing not to be offended by something that's offensive to somebody else. Sure, I could accept the grown men who didn't find themselves affected by the shirt, but they were never really the demographic that I was concerned for.

As the father of a little girl, I find myself much more attuned to these things, much more sensitive about them, and to be honest, I feel a little bit ashamed of that. I've always been a feminist intellectually, politically, but I feel like I shouldn't have needed to have a little girl to become one viscerally. Did having a daughter change your politics at all? It's a conversation that I've had with Wayde, and I know he felt his feminism in a way he never had before after having Senna. Are we wrong? Shouldn't we have been there the whole time?

Anyhow, when I got home, I was properly choked up and teary and gave Joséphine an embarrassing little speech about how we were going to fix the world for her, clean it up so that she'd have a clear take-off. I need to get these speeches in now, before she can remember them, before she understands them and has to roll her eyes at how dramatic and overwrought her father is being.

But I can't think about the world without thinking of her anymore. This week, the US and China surprised everyone by announcing a bilateral climate-change agreement, and interestingly, my thoughts moved in the opposite way than they usually would in a situation like that. Instead of being euphoric at the news, then slowly becoming more realistically despondent, I initially reacted with cynicism before warming to the announcement and then letting myself think: "Wait a minute, does this mean her world is going to be okay?"

With love, and a promise not to lag this long again,
Charlie

Toronto, November 30, 2014 (i.e., a day before my birthday, hint hint)

Dear junior dad,

I am in Toronto, where it is cold, as one would expect, while you are in Vancouver, where my Facebook correspondents brag about the cold and snow, some claiming centimetres, others claiming millimetres. You are at stand-up church with your baby daughter, nice and warm. My daughter is in Edmonton, and I have not heard any of my Facebook friends in Edmonton mention the weather, as who would? Do people in Saskatchewan comment on the flatness of the terrain?

Don't think for a minute that I am going to fall for your Nilometer baloney. I say "baloney" only because I can't think of the right word for an intellectual comparison of a semi-metaphorical nature. Oh, and it was just now that I twigged to the fact that Nilometer is named after the river. The Nile fascinated me when I was a kid, so long before you were a kid. A few years ago Jean and I crossed the Nile in a bus. It was like a river, you know? Another river.

Just the opposite of you. You are not just another father-and-daughter combo. You can tell that by the hundreds of Facebook messages you get after you post a picture of you and your smiling progeny. Sort of like Mary and Jesus, I suppose—iconic. So don't fret overmuch about being so tardy with your last letter. But start on the next one right away; it's my birthday tomorrow. I'm not getting any younger. Or mail.

I am impressed by your killing workload, and I respect all you're doing, partly because I sympathize. I won't say anything about the nine books I have coming out in the next couple years, or the fact that there will be ten if you get on your horse, because I have Jean, who does everything for me except press the keys on this keyboard. But I remember the first years of the seventies, when I was writing and editing books, groaning at SFU, running a magazine, travelling back and forth across the country, doing stuff on CBC, writing reviews, cooking, washing, mowing, changing diapers, not to mention holding down the shortstop position for the Granville Grange Zephyrs. I honestly can't remember what Gumpy was like when I was disappearing to Burnaby or Fredericton, or coming back from, say, Windsor. I do remember that I worried about her while I was away, and there was no such thing as Facebook, and I couldn't afford to telephone long distance. I might have shed a tear or so, though I am not the blubbermouth you are. You young hipsters are so damned sensitive.

Ain't they wonderful, though? I mean years. I am so much looking forward to your Christmas Panto this year. It will be the first one that Joji has seen, though I guess that she heard last year's while inside the human carrying case she was satisfied to stay in. Next year she will probably perform in the Panto. At this point I should let you know that I have been wondering why you haven't asked me to strut or fly across the stage.

Referring to your last letter, I want to report that there's a note on my hard copy saying that this is the funniest line I have heard and imagine some comedian saying: "That decision should pay off big time next year when our family is, you know, eating groceries and living in a place." You ought to get a job as a master of ceremonies. Do you still have your Mortimer Snerd? When I was a little kid, my ambition was to grow up some and sit on Mr Bergen's lap. (This was a lead-up to a wonderful comic climax, but someone just turned on the TV, and I can't remember it.) I listened to a show about a ventriloquist—on the radio! Uh.

I liked hearing about your trip *en famille* to Whistler. I hope you got pictures of my little namesake getting held in the arms of all the illustrious writers. I am glad to have whatever pictures we have of Thea with all the poor and famous. I will keep them forever, even if

I sell copies to the magazines. You want me to come over and hold your kid while you snap the camera or whatever it is you young folks do to make pictures?

Anyway, I used to tell the kid what a grind it was, touring the snow country, sleeping on basement couches, running to catch the bus to Thistleweed, Manitoba. I would pant and sniffle and fall into a chair, asking whether I could sit for a bit before I started making the meatloaf. Then, a month or so after her mother died, I asked Thea, who had just turned twenty-eight, to come along with me for my appearances at the Toronto writers' festival. They gave me a suite in a big US hotel down at the lake front—giant fluffy towels, giant fluffy dressing gowns, bars of soap that were bigger than the ones we had at home. She arched an eyebrow at me.

"Honest," I said. "I never get this kind of treatment."

It was a sad time. Maybe that's why I was so proud of her when she moved to the other end of the long table at the French restaurant to get away from the British poet laureate, a pain in the ass who could not write his way out of a wet paper stanza.

That's interesting, that question about becoming a girl's father and one's politics. I always feel a little funny calling myself a feminist, but I have always felt terrible associating with sexist assholes. When I was eight I got my picture taken wearing half my aunt Pam's army uniform (even if she wasn't a famous writer), and in grade four, I played on the girls' side of the school instead of the boys' side. However, or maybe so, I don't recall a shift in my politics upon becoming a father. Maybe there was one, but mainly I remember how fiercely protective I got. Not that suspiciously he-man kind of protective that fathers get against would-be boyfriends (one jokes about that), but the protective one feels against a *world* that wants to make life hard for girls and women. Maybe that's why I made sure that my girl kid got a sawed-off hockey stick. I feel that way about Joji, too. No one better give her a copy of *Atlas Shrugged*.

But you have to watch this, too. If it turns out that your daughter likes to wear pink clothes and wants pink bed sheets and pink toys and a Barbie with pink cheeks, it isn't a great idea to take away the pink stuff or make fun of it and buy her a big yellow plastic backhoe. It is true that I outfitted my kid in Wonder Woman pyjamas, but you have to think about that, too. I know that WW lassoes bad men and sometimes socks them, but couldn't it be possible that she is some male comics-author's somewhat complicated fantasy?

I don't know. But I do know this, my sometimes slightly neurotic friend: our Joji is in good hands. She's so lucky to have been born to the couple she inherited. She might have to eat some weird stuff from unconventional grocery stores, but I know that her dad and I will take her to baseball games sometimes, and she can watch me eat a double chili dog.

Your biggest fan, except when you tell the boilsucker joke,
GB

December 19, 2014

Dear Pops,

I am writing you today—just six days before my daughter's first Christmas, three days before what would have been her first birthday if she'd arrived on her due date—with a low-grade headache and a bit more self-consciousness than usual. I'm not self-conscious because the letter's late; it's not too bad this time, really, just over two weeks, although I'm sorry I didn't write you one on your birthday (I guess we hipsters aren't *that* sensitive), but because I recently read an interview with the very good writer Jenny Diski, who very tragically has been diagnosed with terminal cancer and who is writing about it. She said this about her project: "I was concerned by the 'Oh God, not another cancer diary' thing. What could be worse? Only another 'new father diary' maybe ..." Gulp.

But we don't have anything to worry about on that score, do we? This isn't a diary, right? It's a correspondence. When you write into a diary, it doesn't write back in the voice of a sassy seventy-nine-year-old guy from Oliver, does it? Okay, maybe I am sensitive.

So, the headache: For several nights, more than I can keep track of, I have been sleeping downstairs on our leather couch in order to let mother and daughter sleep next to each other on our bed, so that the former can keep close tabs on the latter. Joji sleeping alongside us is nothing new, of course—she usually gets brought in for a few hours a night, at least, against prevailing medical wisdom as well as parental sleeping comfort. But for the past few weeks, our little girl has been snotty, coldy, coughy, croupy, and sometimes feverish. (I have learned this week that there is no sound which packs more pathos than one's own little baby coughing until she gags.) Temporarily, it has become Cara and Joséphine's bedroom, which I visit now and then. Last night, the whole family woke up together at about five-thirty in the morning to watch a 38.7-degree fever and try to get it down. Eventually, it abated, and we then all went back to sleep until noon. Hence a workday nearly lost for me, plus a long headache to go with it. For what it's worth, the baby's croup was the proximate cause for the errand which made me feel more like a father than almost anything else I've done: going to the twenty-four-hour pharmacy in the middle of the night to buy a humidifier. And, for the record, a bag of liquorice.

Otherwise, it has mostly been a good month—for starters, and importantly, we have finally secured daycare for next month, when Cara returns to paid work. (See, that's a feminist way of phrasing it, which also happens to be accurate—incidentally, out of curiosity, why do you have trouble identifying as a feminist? Because you stand to pee? We're allowed in the club too, George.) We were worried there, for a while. Although Joji has been on a dozen or so public daycare waitlists since she was a zygote, Vancouver's notorious shortage of spaces sent us looking into private, home daycare possibilities. If you ever want to test whether your danger-seeking antennae are in working order, try heading to a stranger's house to figure out if it's some place you'd want to leave your helpless, non-verbal child (but I should add, verbiage-wise, that the kiddo has now taken to crawling up to Dad's feet when she wants to be lifted, pointing skyward, and saying something that sounds very, very close to "Up"). The first place we went was run by a very sweet, older Bosnian woman, but the place was small, it was on a busy street (and one of her legally mandated two gates was open when we first arrived), and there was a pot of steaming water close to the edge of the counter. It didn't help my anxiety, of course, that it was such an emotionally fraught circumstance to begin with. For a few minutes, the woman took Joji into the playroom with the three little kids she was looking after while Cara and I sat in the other room looking at paperwork. As you've noted, Joséphine is a charismatic little girl and not just on Facebook. As the daycare owner held Joji in her lap, the other children brought her toys, almost in fealty, and our girl seemed happy and satisfied as can be, and she shot me a wholly independent and ready-for-the-world look over her shoulder that just about wrecked me.

In the end, we found a very nice Afghani woman who will take Joji three days a week. She works in her home-based hair salon the other two days (she has pretty great hair). This woman is kind but very no-nonsense, with almost no nervousness in her energy at all, which calmed all three of us so far as I can tell. At one point, I was looking at a layout/map of her house that she had on the wall, with one room labelled the "bad room." I was confused and asked if that's where children went for time-outs. She said no, it's better just to speak with the children. That seemed sensible to me, but I still couldn't figure out what went on in the bad room until Cara quietly pointed out that it was likely a misspelling of "bedroom."

Another occasion that I had to feel properly fatherly this month was when I took Joséphine down to the Stanley Park Christmas Train with our pals Wayde Compton and Ryan Knighton and their little girls. The train having been a long-time tradition over the course of my own childhood, I was beaming with pride to be making like my own dear dad and taking my little one to see it—except that, even though we got there at six p.m. we were too late to get on any train before the older girls' bedtimes. After milling around for a while partially stupefied by defeat, Wayde's and Ryan's girls eating popcorn and candy canes as a sop, we vowed to try again next week, this time reserving tickets online before we go.

I'm a big fan of the month of December, George. Not only does it kick off with your birthday, but it's also my wedding anniversary on the ninth, and this year, as last year, it's Panto month—and, of course, there's Christmas.

The Panto's going well this year, though we scuttled our plans to bring Joji—I still may try to sneak her in before closing. I did bring her to part of one of the rehearsals, at which Veda and the whole cast sang for her an impromptu rendition of "Do-Re-Mi," to her moderate delight. That same afternoon, she refused to leave my arms as I did an interview in the lobby with French CBC, and so this month also saw my little girl's big TV debut. I was interviewed by a journalist whom I find very, very beautiful and who was fawning so completely over Joséphine that I asked her if she had children, and when her "No" arrived sounding full of regret, I felt terrible for having asked.

The reviews and, I think, the sales for this year's Panto are even better than last year's, which has been cause for joy, but the opening was marked by some minor tension with a friend that got grossly blown out of proportion in my own head and was the spark for several days' worth of despairing. The month, one of my favourites of the year, kicked off with several days' worth of deep, unshakeable blues—the (hopefully) rare kind in which a person sometimes thinks about how much easier everything would have been if they'd never been born, or if, having been born, could now just gently let go. I've had more than my fair share of thoughts like this over the years, but it's interesting the way they change now that I, having been saddled with this ambiguous gift/burden of life, have now passed it along to somebody else. A comedian I know, John Beuhler, once sent out a tweet to the effect that having children was a good way to take suicide off the table. His post was very dark and more than a little cynical, but there's truth in it.

Did I know that Thea had lost her mother? I can't remember if I did, and I'm ashamed to say that. There's nothing worse in the world than losing one's mother, at least nothing that I've experienced. It's now part of what will always keep me obstinately breathing through those moments in which I'd rather not be. Having grown up missing a parent, I couldn't ever stick Joséphine with the same thing. Which probably means fewer bags of liquorice too, while we're on the subject.

The clouds cleared after a few days, and I have mostly been able to enjoy the beginnings of Baby's First Christmas. We have yet to have a sitting with Santa Claus for a proper photo, but I did snap a quick one on my phone of Joji looking warily up at our neighbour Sheldon, who was dressed as the Big Man for our housing co-op Christmas party last week. Yesterday afternoon, I picked up an eight-dollar, foot-and-a-half-tall artificial tree—"the deadbeat dad Christmas tree" as I described it to the unimpressed cashier at Wonderbucks, who nevertheless let me take the display model replete with a few decorative bells because he said it'd be too much trouble to take them off—that now sits on our dining room table, where it can announce to the world that it is Christmas without being accessible to little hands or a little mouth. I decorated it yesterday with one hand, cradling the baby in the crook of my arm, while a song from *How the Grinch Stole Christmas* played over the computer and Cara took a shower. Joséphine watched impassively as I hung the ornaments—a 2014 "My First Christmas" bauble sent by my grandmother in Ste. Thérèse, hanging close by my 1980 "Baby's First Christmas" ball, a 2007 "Our First Christmas Together" up near my parents' from 1979—until the Angel who sat atop the Christmas trees of my childhood took her place once more at the apex of ours. Finally, Joséphine smiled.

Merry Christmas, George.

Love,
C.

Dear Smiley,

I was so looking forward to your Christmas letter, and so happy that it arrived before Christmas. I need all the help I can get this time of year. You should have been here to cheer me up this morning. I always get low this time of year, and sure enough, when I turned on my new digital radio system this morning and switched from classical music to jazz while reading the newspaper and doing the *New York Times* crossword, all the jazz stations were playing jazz versions of Christmas songs. I tried the blues stations, and learned that there are Christmas blues songs. I am betting that the rock stations and folk stations and cowboy stations were playing seasonal ditties. Some hockey-jersey-wearing hiphopper was probably vocalizing a rap fa-la-la-la-la. I was wishing that you were over here doing an ironic "hipster" stand-up routine about the frustrations and anxiety of Christmas.

It's a good thing that Jean and I don't do anything about Noël except hang our X-rated wreath on the front door.

But I believe that the topic was baby daughter's first Christmas. Well, Thea's first Christmas took place in our ex-commune on York Street. She was two-and-a-half months old, so what she mainly did was attach her face to her mother's similar-sized breast, with time-outs for baby-barf and baby-poop. We had just arrived back in town after a family visit to Oliver, and Kerrisdale roofs and yards and streets were covered with Christmas snow. Our friend Tony had arrived Christmas Eve from Calgary. I had been working for days and nights at the dining room table, reading 125 full applications for Canada Council grants, wondering how I had slipped and fallen into the Establishment. Every once in a while I would make sure to have a look at Gumpy because she was doing something new every day. The crooked little mouth that was once her smile was now replaced by a huge one that lit up her face. And she was often looking around for her mom, really lighting up when she spotted her.

But really, her first Christmas came in 1972, when she was a year and a bit old. Now we five (counting Frank the dog and Small, his dog) were in our first non-rented house, on Balaclava between Broadway and 10th. On the corner of Balaclava and 10th, there was the solid thump of an automobile collision every day.

(December 24)

Despite my usual late-December depression, I was making some propitiations to Christmas. In my upstairs writing room, I wrote in my diary that downstairs there was a sheaf of bills that I had written cheques for, to try to shave them a bit, but Mrs Bowering advised against mailing said cheques until after the new year; a cheque I was supposed to get from the CBC was late, and anyway it was not going to help pay for the things I had imagined it would help pay for because now there were more unimagined things that were saying "Ahem" more often and louder. Meanwhile, the ceiling in Gumpy's room was leaking, and we didn't have the funds to get it fixed.

But the dishwasher had arrived, though I was content to continue washing dishes by hand. And we got a Christmas tree, poor little thing, and put it up on top of one the big stereo speakers, with a chair in front of it, hoping to prevent the Gump from pulling it over on herself. Angela was, on the other hand, looking forward to seeing her rip her presents open on Christmas morn. I had a pain behind my left eyeball, as if I had been drinking the night before, but all I had been doing was watching an Alistair Sim movie on TV.

Then, as it will, Christmas arrived on the twenty-fifth, our first

Christmas as home owners. It was a funny place, that house on Bala-clava. I have mentioned that some previous loser had decided to turn it into a duplex, but then ran out of steam or money or someone tipped him or the city off, and questions of zoning and licences got asked. There were two front doors, one of which I tried in my amateur dad way to insulate, which made it impossible to open. There were things coming out of the walls upstairs that were probably meant to connect with future stoves and toilets and so on. The bedroom we were using on the main floor had been designed as a dining room.

On Christmas Day it poured rain from morning to night, but little Thea celebrated happily, tearing colourful wrappings off a lot of toys and clothing—and singing. She had recently learned how to sing, and was the possessor of a lovely musical voice. At the same time her dancing had become quite complex. When she danced and sang she usually had an abstracted concentrating look, and at that time looked remarkably like her mother, who had, as a girl, a fantasy about being a torch singer. C.J. Newman, the novelist, said that if she was still so musical next year we ought to get her into that Suzuki violin system. In a pre-Christmas party over at Warren and Ellen Tallman's house, she played the piano quite beautifully, I thought. She liked Sonny and Cher's singing on their TV show, but I thought she was better than they.

Christmas night, Angela telephoned everyone she knew who lived elsewhere, and Thea sang while playing with Christmas wrap-pings, while I completely forgot to take pictures. Well, that involved buying rolls of film for the camera. We sentimentally got Thea into her crib placed carefully to avoid the leak in her ceiling, and watched her sleeping with one of her new cloth animals.

Then, from midnight until three in the morning, I bailed rainwa-ter out of the basement. I longed for a midnight clear.

On the twenty-seventh, it was a sunny day, mainly. Thea's local grandmother had given her a bird-feeding house for Christmas, and I put it up out front where Angela wanted it because Thea spent so much time on the couch under the front window. But the birds didn't come near the corn and sunflower seeds. They were busy working on the shrivelled fruit on the plum tree in the back yard.

(December 25)

About being a feminist: I am ninety-five-percent sure that I am wrong about this, but though I support and cheer for feminist causes, I am too embarrassed to call myself a feminist, as if that would be presumptive. I feel like a billionaire calling himself a socialist. Like the wealthy Chinese kids in my neighbourhood saying "yo" to each other and tagging all the garage doors with the expensive spray paint they bought with a credit card. I support the Rasta cause in its more progressive ambitions, but I would not wear light-grey dreadlocks if I could grow them. I am not much impressed by those white Toronto basketball fans holding up their "We The North" signs. I wish that Libby Davies were premier of BC, and that Christy Clark were working at Value Village.

Oh, and I stand to pee only half the time.

Which reminds me of a neat memory about Thea from when she was about three. She was an attendee of a co-op daycare for kids too young for regular daycare. Her main companion there was an African boy who was just a bit older, Roger by name. She imitated him in everything. For a while we put up with her standing to pee as best she could in the upstairs toilet. Cute, we said, but probably psychologically unadvised. Angela took a lot of advice from shrinks.

So the kid used to make my heart trip quite often. But so do you, as when you write about the "wholly independent and ready-for-the-world look over [Joji's] shoulder that just about wrecked" you.

(December 25)

I think of the Stanley Park miniature train often, but I haven't been there in a long time. Didn't I hear a few years ago that they had closed it down? I am so glad that it is still running. Gosh, those things are fun. Was the engineer all done up in one of those engineer outfits, grey-and-white striped coveralls and cap, such as I used to play ball in? I remember taking little Thea there and then to the nearby petting zoo, where her favourite creatures were the pigeons. It was always this way at the park, and once I had got past the momentary disappointment, I taught myself to be proud of this kid. I think that she first tipped us off about this by playing with her Christmas gift wrappers more than her toys.

One Stanley Park memory that won't let go of me had to do with the refreshments stand. Angela's old-time friend Heather was up from Tampa with her two kids, and I took them all to the Park. While Sam and Louisa were slurping on their Coca Colas, the little Gump had to make do with apple juice. This was the Vancouver way we were raising her. As you can imagine, I had mixed feelings about this day too.

It wasn't so much, by the way, Thea's having lost her mom. It was Thea's watching her mom dying, both in the sense of years of MS and fewer years of cancer operations, and then finally being in the room when Angela breathed her last. Thea wasn't a little kid; she was in her late twenties. Just about the time a daughter starts noticing her own adulthood and is ready for long womanly conversations with her mother. Now she has compiled a lot of research, including her mother's own research, and is writing a book about that mother and that daughter, trying to get the conversation going that way. I hope that I'll manage to live long enough to read it.

In a sense, I guess she's doing the same thing that we are doing, but doing it the other way round.

Then there is the experience of the mother who actually got these letters about our daughters going. Jean "lost her daughter" one night on a highway thousands of kilometres away. She could have written a book about that, another candidate for "nothing worse in the world," but she edited one instead, and a lot of people who needed that book got it. It's called *The Heart Does Break,* and it's still in print.

Here I am, writing on Christmas Day, as I have done all my adult life. There's a danger of getting maudlin while writing on Christmas Day, and I hope I haven't been, too much. There is sunlight coming through the Venetian blind, making me squint. Makes me want to try for treacly instead of maudlin.

What the heck. When I was a kid I knew enough not to expect extravagance on Christmas Day. The aunts and uncles were plenty.

Some kind of holiday—
GB

January 27, 2015

Dear Jorge,

You are in Mexico at the moment, sipping Ovaltine beachside, while I am here at home, in an unseasonably warm pocket of Canadian winter. I've been meaning to write for the last several days, at least, but plans to do so kept getting scuttled by various obstacles: a doctor's appointment for Joséphine, other deadlines, in-the-marrow exhaustion—all of which raise the question of my suitability to be the co-author of a book about being a dad. Today, the writing plans were almost set aside again, this time due to circumstances that raise the question of my suitability to be a dad in the first place.

I am thirty-four years old, I am a working professional, I am somebody's father—and today, BC Hydro cut off the power to our home because I hadn't paid my bills. Not only had I not paid my bills, but I had failed to register the myriad notices, by post and by phone, that I had apparently received warning me of this possibility. So clueless was I about this basic, adult responsibility that this afternoon, when the power went out while I was alone in the house, I didn't wince and say, "Fuck, the Hydro bill!"; I thought, *Hm, a power outage, how inconvenient*, before taking a shower by candlelight in a bid to get ready for work. Only when I found out, via Facebook, that none of my neighbours had lost their juice did it occur to me to go through the pile of unread (never to be read, unreadable) mail on the ledge by the front door to find a letter sent by BC Hydro on January 9, informing me of $517.09 past due. "Collection action may include service disconnection," it said. "You are responsible for protecting your premises from possible damages caused by freezing." It didn't say anything about the little girl whom I'm supposed to help keep warm too.

All of this was sheer negligence on my part; we're not hard up for cash, just for the time it takes to go through the mail and pay bills over the computer. Which made my pleading phone call to the woman who was to arrange our reconnection all the more humiliating. The house was already growing cold, even as the fridge and freezer were warming up, and the air unseasonably warm or not, I didn't want our little Joji—who has been coughing with such a tubercular hack (that she caught from me) that she's been gagging, and having trouble sleeping nights—to have to be huddled up after sundown. None of my begging or special pleading or insolent and obnoxious excuse-making ("Why wasn't I sent a notice?!") were of any use, and I was simply informed that the reconnection team would try to reconnect today if they could (at this point there was only about an hour left in their workday), but that if the power wasn't back on by five, we should try to make arrangements for somewhere else to stay. At that point—after having run through the house unplugging every single thing that plugs in, in preparation for the reconnection—I had to leave for my class, feeling entirely the shitty, failed, undeserving father. Happily, a little while later, I got a text from Cara saying that we were in the clear. The lamps, heat, stove, fridge, and lights work again. My daughter has been spared any knowledge that her old man's an idiotic, disorganized deadbeat—at least until she's old enough to read this.

It's January, a new year and a month full of firsts, including, this past weekend, the kiddo's first haircut, performed by yours truly, in three quick but expert snips on a whim at our friends' place. This was a big deal for me, because my dad was our haircutter (he even took the tip of my ear off once in the downstairs bathroom), and I think I did a fairly good job of shortening the long, stringy bangs that were crawling down into her eyes and leaving her with a somewhat inelegant mullet ("inelegant mullet" being something of a redundancy) that she can pull off because of that exquisite and kissable face she's got. I took her swimming this month too—which was not technically a first, but a first time in a public pool—not an easy feat for me, because I hate to be shirtless around anybody with eyes, but it was our friends' daughter's fourth birthday. We swam for a while, Joji still wearing four Band-Aids from her one-year immunization shots, and it was pure pleasure for me, while seemingly a mixed experience for her. For some reason, I didn't ask Cara for help with our post-swim wash and change, which I would come to regret. While holding on to a slippery wet baby while standing on a slippery wet tile floor, I somehow managed to get us both undressed, even passably washed and showered, and me into boxer shorts and a T-shirt, when suddenly I felt the spreading, warm wetness of a post-shower pee against my stomach, into the fabric of my T-shirt. Without thinking, after I took off the T-shirt, I rinsed us off once more—soaking the boxers that I had forgotten to remove. I spent the rest of the birthday party without my undershirt or any underwear at all.

Anyway, it's January—and I didn't begin the month or year by my family's side, but rather in a hotel room all by myself in Victoria. I'd been hired for a show over there, and the pay was pretty good, and we figured that New Year's Eve wasn't a big night for babies, and so why not take the gig? As you'll remember, last New Year's Eve, Cara had just received the balloon behind her cervix to begin induction; we had, as I've described, the moment of what I still believe to have been our profoundest, most romantic, and melancholic connection—lying alone in a bed and in a home that would imminently no longer be just ours. That intimacy of last year was traded in for a solitary room at the Ramada, just above the sports bar where I'd been performing (and, it should be said, where I had a very good show, though I was upstairs and between the sheets by 11:15 p.m.). I had hoped to do the countdown with Cara, over the phone, but she was putting the baby to sleep. It was a quiet, lonely, not altogether unpleasant but not altogether happy way to ring in 2015.

A few days later, January 3, was our darling girl's very first birthday. The first birthday is somewhat mythical in my family, because my brother's, in September 1984, had been videotaped with a cutting-edge camcorder rented from our local 7-Eleven. The images were recorded mostly for the sake of relatives in Quebec—"*Bienvenue, à la fête de Nicholas,*" my mother says in a warmly exaggerated, theatrical way, in a language that she doesn't speak. After repeated instructions to say something "to Quebec," the four-year-old me turns up to my father, whose lap I'm sitting on, and asks him sincerely, "Is Quebec in the camera?"—but were cherished in our house, growing up. After Mom was gone, these were some of the few moving pictures that we had of her, some of the few snippets of her voice (like her quietly admonishing my Auntie Laurie for saying to my brother, while the camera was rolling, "the birthday boy's got snot in his nose!," or her singing the theme for *Candid Camera* to my granny as the latter sat in her chair, alternately rolling her eyes and failing to suppress a smile).

The day of Joji's birthday party began with my trip out to the suburbs to Costco to pick up the meats, cheese, and other giant quantities of various things for those on our expansive guest list to eat. "It really is a Hellscape," said my friend Derrick, whose membership we were using, as he took in the scene at the cash registers, and was it ever, though I felt bad thinking it because I remember my mom quite loved Costco, and the day after she died, our neighbour Gail had offered, through tears, that she was at the big Costco in the sky. Or maybe my dad said that. I can't be sure.

For the party we had rented a large room in the community

centre by our house, overlooking Trout Lake, and it was all perfect except that someone had left something rotting in the fridge in the adjacent kitchen, and the odor was so powerfully disgusting that if the fridge door was ajar for even five seconds, the whole kitchen area smelled like a crime scene. You couldn't be there, George, because of a pain in your neck, and a few others couldn't make it, but otherwise we were surrounded by nearly all of our favourite people who live in the city, and it was wonderful. We even had a technological flourish: a virtual-grandfather corner in which my dad and stepdad were wired in to the party by FaceTime, plugged through the speakers, with guests going over to pay respects or chit-chat across the country. Dad and Dwight said the set-up made them feel a bit like Statler and Waldorf, the two cantankerous old men in the balcony of *The Muppet Show*, but they got a huge kick out of it and so did everyone else. We sang "Happy Birthday," then, after my Auntie Laurie reminded me, we sang the personalized version of "*Gens du pays*" that we always used to sing at birthdays when I was a kid ("*Ma chère Joséphine, c'est à ton tour, de te laisser parler d'amour ...*"). My only disappointment was that my little girl didn't make a mess with her piece of cake, which I'd always sort of considered a rite of passage.

I'm out in my office at UBC right now, and my writing of that last paragraph was interrupted by a FaceTime call from Cara and Joji, this time only across town. I won't be getting home before she's asleep, which means that our only contact today will have been the smooch that I gave her while I was half-asleep before she and her mother were out the door. This is only partly alleviated by the fact that we've spent a lot of daddy-daughter time together over the past few days. I miss her when I'm at work, and it's incredible how easy it is to fall into that cliché that one's always seeing or reading or hearing about but never thinks will be them: the dad who misses out on time with his child to do work outside the home that he doesn't love nearly as much as he does her. It's the kind of cliché that you'd think you'd see coming, it's so clanging and clumsy and obvious, but you don't. Or, I didn't.

Cara too is back at work—and absolutely loves it. If she feels any guilt, it is only that she feels no guilt, only exhilaration. Well, that's not entirely true; every day, around three p.m., she begins to really miss the baby. Then she goes to pick her up from daycare (Cara drops her off on all three days; I pick her up on Mondays, Cara gets her Tuesdays and Wednesdays, since I'm teaching). Daycare, too, is going swimmingly, especially now that we've sorted out the small detail of the child's name.

In the week before we started dropping her off for full days with Shala, her daycare worker, Cara went with her mom, who was in town, for a few visits. During the visit, Cara's mom quietly pointed out to Cara that Shala appeared to be calling the baby "Jasmine." Cara, though, was somehow convinced—and even more improbably, managed to convince her mom—that this was not the case, but was just a function of Shala's Afghani accent, that in some inexplicable way "Jo-sé-phine" was coming out sounding like "Jas-ah-meen." When I went to pick up the kid on her first afternoon, it was clear as day that she was being called Jasmine—but now I had no idea how to broach the subject; since nobody had corrected her, I figured now we'd sound crazy if we did. That evening, as we were trying to figure out how to solve the dilemma, we got our chance to clear things up (which we took): Shala called us ecstatically to tell us that she'd found a second baby girl for the daycare, which she'd been looking for, and could we believe it, "she's named Jasmine too!"

It's been over a year now, and I love being a dad more than anything (that is, just as much as I love being married to her mom), and I am desperately, helplessly exhausted in the marrow of my bones, and I am coming to terms with the irrelevance of that exhaustion—of the fact that it just doesn't factor in.

I was worried, as you remember, about the world that she was coming into. Two days ago, in Greece, they elected the socialists, Syriza, and I've been on air, politically, ever since. More than a few lefties I know have been quick to throw water on everyone's hopes for Syriza. Then, when I see the crowds in Greece or the newly elected prime minister, I wonder if we aren't making those first, shaky, baby-deer steps into sturdiness.

I am still routinely flabbergasted that we have a baby, that's she's real. I watch her crawling evolve (there is a dainty, hip-swivelling method and a butch, bulldog, devil-may-care shoulder-driven method), or I watch her picking raisins or Cheerios out of a dish, lifting them between her thumb and index finger, feeding them into her mouth, and then chewing (I could watch her eat forever, I promise). I can't get past the fact that when Cara came down the stairs in April 2013 with a pregnancy test and a happily bemused and slightly disbelieving look on her face that this kid was who she was talking about. If I never fully process that idea? If I'm never completely able to keep it from seeming surreal and fanciful? I'll be okay with that.

Love,
Charlie

Readers' Club Questions:

How do you think the story and the baby would have turned out differently if she had been named Georgina instead of Joséphine?

Do you think that Joji will one day become Prime Minister of Canada? If so, what party will she lead?

Which of the two fathers would you like to see in pyjamas? Why?

George was born in the middle of the Great Depression, and Charlie is a post-boomer child, whatever they are called. How on earth did these two guys become friends?

George maintains that Charlie is neurotic. Charlie claims that Charlie is neurotic. Which one is right? Discuss.

Compare and contrast anything you want to.

Do you think that George should have joined the Velvet Underground rather than trying to be a writer? What kind of father would he have turned out to be?

It has been suggested that the smartest dad in the book is Charlie's father. Do you agree with this peculiar notion? If so, explain yourself.

Could Charlie use a makeover?

Would you like to pre-order Cara's side of the story now?

GEORGE BOWERING is Canada's first poet laureate and an officer of the Order of Canada. He is the author of more than eighty books of fiction, non-fiction, and poetry, the most recent of which include *The Hockey Scribbler, Writing the Okanagan,* and *10 Women.* A native of British Columbia, he lives in Vancouver.

CHARLES DEMERS is a comedian, performer, and writer who often appears on CBC Radio's "The Debaters." His previous books are the non-fiction books *The Horrors* (Douglas & McIntyre) and *Vancouver Special* (Arsenal Pulp Press) and the novel *The Prescription Errors* (Insomniac Press). He lives in Vancouver, where he teaches writing at the University of British Columbia.